GOD'S GENERALS

FOR KIDS

SMITH WIGGLESWORTH

GOD'S GENERALS

FOR KIDS

SMITH WIGGLESWORTH

BY
ROBERTS LIARDON
& OLLY GOLDENBERG

BRIDGE
LOGOS

Newberry, FL 32669

Bridge-Logos

Newberry, Florida 32669 USA

God's Generals For Kids—Smith Wigglesworth

Roberts Liardon & Olly Goldenberg

Copyright ©2013 Roberts Liardon & Olly Goldenberg

Second Edition

Printed in the United States of America.

Library of Congress Catalog Card Number 2018908595

International Standard Book Number: 978-1-61036-474-4

International Standard Book Number Hardcover: 978-1-61036-232-0

International Standard Book Number Large Print: 978-1-61036-244-3

Unless otherwise noted, all Scripture is from the King James Version of the Bible.

The photographs used are owned by and taken from the private collection of Roberts Liardon.

Timeline illustrations by David Parfitt.

SMITH WIGGLESWORTH

CONTENTS

TIMELINE

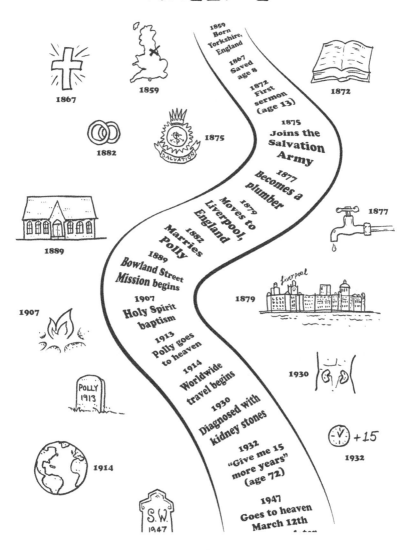

1867

1859

1872

1882

1875

1889

1907

POLLY 1913

1914

S.W. 1947

1859
Born Yorkshire, England

1867
Saved age 8

1872
First sermon (age 13)

1875
Joins the Salvation Army

1877
Becomes a plumber

1879
Moves to Liverpool, England

1882
Marries Polly

1889
Bowland Street Mission begins

1907
Holy Spirit baptism

1913
Polly goes to heaven

1914
Worldwide travel begins

1930
Diagnosed with kidney stones

1932
"Give me 15 more years" (age 72)

1947
Goes to heaven March 12th

1877

1879

1930

1932
+15

CHAPTER 1

GROWING UP POOR

Four Generations

LIFE AT HOME

Life is hard for some children. You probably know you will get a tasty meal each day, and you probably have toys to play with. But not every child has that. In Smith Wigglesworth's family they had none of these things.

Smith's family was very poor. They lived in Yorkshire County, in a town called Menston, in England.

Smith's father and mother, John and Martha Wigglesworth, did their very best to provide for their three sons and one daughter. But they didn't have enough money and couldn't afford to buy clothes, so the kind people in Menston would give the Wigglesworths their old clothes when they didn't need them anymore. Then Smith's mother would cut up these old clothes and use the material to make "new" shirts, pants, dresses, and so on. She sometimes made Smith's shirtsleeves too long, but he didn't mind because the extra long sleeves kept his hands warm during the cold winters in England.

Feeding their family was very difficult for Smith's father and mother. They couldn't afford to go out to eat at restaurants. After all, you can't eat "out" when you can barely afford to eat "in." Here is what was for dinner most nights at Smith's home: Potatoes, more potatoes, and bread.

Once in a while, the family had enough money to go to the store and buy a piece of fatty bacon that no one else wanted. That was a real treat for Smith and his brothers and sister. You may think a lump of fat and a bit of bacon may not sound like much of a treat, but to Smith it was delicious and amazing!

Even though Smith's mother and father were poor, they loved their children. When Smith was born, on Wednesday,

June 8, 1859, his parents were really happy to have another baby in the family. But they did worry…"How are we going to be able to look after our growing family?" His mother wondered aloud. "We just don't have enough money."

Now, Smith's father worked really hard to earn as much money as he could. But he didn't have a regular job and had to find part-time work and odd jobs wherever he could. Unfortunately, on some of these jobs, he worked very long workdays for very little pay.

When Smith's mother worried about money, his father would comfort her, saying, "We'll do what we've always done Martha. We'll take it one day at a time and share with each other whatever we can afford to eat."

IT'S A HARD LIFE

One winter, Smith's father was hired to dig a ditch. Unfortunately, the ground had frozen solid and poor Mr. Wigglesworth felt like he was digging through stone.

"Why don't you wait a week or two to finish this job?" Smith's mother said. "The ground will probably be a bit softer then and it will be much easier to dig the ditch when it's warmer."

"And what will our children eat for the next two weeks?" his father asked.

They both knew he had to do the job right away for they had no money, and there was no more food at home. If Mr. Wigglesworth waited, his family would surely starve. So he went back to digging up the frozen earth. As he worked, he realized he had an audience. A bird perched on a tree above him started singing happily. The little bird helped cheer up Smith's father as he went about his task.

As you can see, Smith's father was a hard worker. But no matter how hard he worked, his family was still poor. When Smith was only six years old, his parents decided that he had to go to work too. They didn't *want* him to work, but they needed him to help out because they simply didn't have enough money to feed a family of six. Everyone in the family was going to have to earn money.

Can you imagine being six years old and having to work all day? Smith was put in a field and told to pick turnips. He worked hard, just like his father. Each morning he woke up early and spent the whole day yanking turnips out of the ground. Then he had to wash the dirt off of them and by the end of the day his small hands were swollen, sore and blistered.

On cold days, the stubborn turnips were really hard to pull out of the ground. It was like having a tug-of-war with a gorilla! On hot days, little 6 year-old Smith would sweat and pant as he toiled under the blazing sun. But he was not allowed to stop working—until lunchtime. Then it was right back to work.

On rainy days, Smith got soaked and shivered from the cold, because he didn't have a nice warm coat to wear.

Now, you might be wondering, "Why weren't Smith and his brothers and sister in school?" Well, according to the law in England in the 1860s, children didn't have to go to school. Boys and girls could attend school but if their families needed them at home or to go to work, they didn't have to go. Even if they didn't like going to school it was better than working all day.

Smith earned a small amount of money picking the turnips, and every bit of his earnings went toward buying food for the family. He didn't get to use any of it for toys or candy. This may sound like a pretty miserable life to you. But to Smith, this was the only life that he knew. He was a brave six-year-old and his life wasn't all bad. While he worked in the fields he loved to look at the world around him. He saw many beautiful flowers, deer, rabbits, and lots of other wildlife. His favorite creatures were birds.

LOVING NATURE

Smith loved birds, just as his father did. Sometimes, he would catch birds and take them home as pets. Before long, the small two-room house was filled with 16 birds, in addition to the six Wigglesworths. Occasionally, when Smith caught a bird he would take it to the market to sell it. But Smith didn't spend any of the money on himself. He gave it to his parents so that they could buy food.

Sometimes, when Smith was out looking for birds, he would ask God to show him a nest. God seemed to answer these prayers because Smith always knew where to look to find a nest full of birds.

Once, Smith found a nest of very tiny birds. He waited a while and didn't see a mother or father bird around. He was afraid that the baby birds had been deserted, so he took the nest full of baby birds home to care for them. After a while, the mother bird flew through an open window, with food for her babies. Smith kept the window open, and the mother bird flew in and out as she pleased to take care of her babies.

It was rather strange for Smith to ask God to help him find birds because his parents were not Christians, and nobody had ever taught Smith to pray. Somehow, he just knew. He prayed throughout each day. He loved to talk to God—and *not* just about birds.

A REGULAR JOB

When Smith turned seven, his father finally found a regular job working in a wool mill. At this mill, sheep's wool was turned into yarn to make clothes. For the very first time, the Wigglesworth family had enough money to buy food and every one of them could go to sleep at night with a full stomach.

Before long, young Smith joined his father working in the mill. Every morning, Smith would wake up at 5:00 a.m. to eat a quick breakfast. By about 5:20, he was out the door, hiking the two miles from his house to the mill because work started at 6 a.m. sharp.

Smith worked for 12 hours every day, Monday through Saturday. He worked 72 hours every week! That's about twice as long as many adults today work at their jobs! And remember, Smith was only 7 years old. At six in the evening, he walked the two miles home to eat supper.

Sunday was the only day he could stay home and rest… but Smith didn't rest on Sundays. Instead, he chose to go to church with his grandmother. That's right—he wanted to go to church more than sleep!

Smith's grandma was a Methodist, and her church had exciting services, with lots of singing and dancing. Smith really enjoyed church. That's why he went every Sunday, even though his parents and brothers and sister didn't come along.

However, even though Smith talked to God all the time and went to church regularly, he didn't feel like he really *knew* God. But that was about to change.

CHAPTER 2

ONLY BELIEVE!

It's all in the Bible

JESUS DIED FOR ME

One Sunday found Smith, now 8 years old, in church as usual. His grandmother was standing next to him, and everybody was singing, clapping, and dancing. Everyone was really excited about Jesus. When they started singing a song about "the blood" of Jesus their praise became even louder.

As Smith watched and listened, something happened inside him. For the first time this little 8-year-old boy named Smith, from a family who was poor and did not know Jesus as their Savior, realized that Jesus had died for *him*. Somehow, Smith understood that God, who sent His Son Jesus to die, wanted something from him. God wanted Smith to believe in Him. He didn't have to do anything complicated. Just believe in God, and His Son, Jesus Christ.

"Was that all he had to do?" you ask. Yes, that was all that Smith had to do because Jesus did everything for Smith and for you and me when He died on the Cross and took our sins away. We were forever forgiven of those sins. In fact, God, Jesus' Father, took those sins and threw them into the sea of forgetfulness to be gone forever.

Then the most wonderful thing happened, Jesus became alive again because He had power over death. When people believe in Jesus and in God, who sent Jesus to Earth to take away our sins, our sins are gone forever. What's more, we get to learn to love God and Jesus and become close friends with them because they love us even more than we know.

Again, what do people have to do? *Only believe.*

Those two words would become very important to Smith. He didn't know it that Sunday when he was only 8, but one day thousands of people all over the world would hear him say. "Only believe. All things are possible—*only believe!*"

On this particular Sunday when 8 year-old Smith believed, he told God, "I believe in you. I believe your Son, Jesus, took the punishment for my sins when He died for me. I believe in you."

When Smith got home, he told his family all about Jesus. Before long, his mother was ready to believe in God too. His father decided to start taking the whole family to church. Smith's father didn't believe in God right away, but, still, he felt it was his duty to take the family to church.

Meanwhile, Smith's life had changed forever. He used to chat casually with God. Now he truly knew God. It was like they were close friends.

A FRIEND OF GOD

One day, while Smith was making his two-mile walk to work, a storm suddenly began. Lightning flashed. Thunder crashed. Smith knew he couldn't run home. He had to get to work, but he was terrified. He cried out, "Help me, God!" and as soon as Smith spoke, his fear vanished. Smith could feel that God was with him and keeping him safe.

At first, young Smith thought everyone truly knew God, just as he did. But, after getting to know a lot of other Christians, he sensed that he was different from most of them. When he was 10, Smith was "confirmed" in the church. (Does your church do confirmations for young people?) At Smith's church, *confirmation* meant promising that you really, truly wanted to follow Jesus. After you proclaimed this, a bishop (church leader) would place his hands on your head or shoulders and pray for you. As the bishop prayed for him, Smith could feel God's love. He felt special inside. He felt peace and love like never before. In fact, he kind of hoped the bishop's prayer would never end. He didn't want to lose this comforting and wonderful feeling.

As soon as the service ended, some of the other newly confirmed children started arguing with each other. Some of them were even swearing. Smith did not want to join in. For the next few days, he could feel God's presence very strongly inside him.

When he saw the other children misbehaving or saying things they shouldn't, he wanted no part of it. No doubt about it, he was a different kind of kid. He felt sure that God had a special plan for his life.

HUNGRY FOR GOD

When Smith was 13, his family moved to Bradford, England. There was a mill there that offered more work than the one in Menston. Smith found a Methodist Church in Bradford and started attending faithfully.

As the days rolled by, he became hungrier and hungrier for God. Because Smith had spent most of his young life working, he had rarely stepped inside of a school. So he had never learned to read. This frustrated him, because he knew the Bible was a very important book, but he could recognize only a few of its words. Still, he carried a New Testament with him wherever he went, even though most of its contents were a mystery to him.

Smith wanted to live for Jesus and wherever he went, he told people about Jesus. He was not shy about his strong beliefs. Most people he talked to just laughed at him. But the mocking didn't discourage Smith. He kept right on talking about Jesus.

Some of the leaders at Smith's church recognized how much this teenager loved God—and how much his faith meant to him. They asked Smith if he would stand up in church and say a few words. "How does three Sundays from now sound?" the pastor asked. For the next three weeks, the nervous 13-year-old prayed and prayed. The big Sunday came. When Smith stood up in front of the church, he felt God's power inside of him. He talked for 15 minutes straight. He was so excited about God and everyone in the congregation could see it. When Smith finished speaking, he couldn't remember the words he had said. But he could tell that everyone had enjoyed listening to him share his love for God. The people in Smith's church loved his enthusiasm. There was something different about the way he talked about God. When Smith was 16, he met a group of people who were as excited about God as he was.

MARCHING IN GOD'S ARMY

In 1875, the Salvation Army marched into town. The Salvation Army is an organization that helps people who are needy. They provide, as one of their mottos says, "Soup, soap, and salvation." Salvation Army members are given ranks, like captain and general, just like in the military army. (You might have seen a Salvation Army member at Christmastime, ringing a bell and collecting money for the poor.)

"We're going to tell everyone about Jesus," some people from the Salvation Army called out to the residents of Bradford. "If you love Jesus, you should give Him your whole life."

Clearly, these people weren't afraid to tell people about Jesus wherever they went.

Finally! Smith said to himself. *Some people who are as excite▪ about Jesus as I am! I know these people can help me grow as a Christian.*

These Salvation Army "soldiers" loved to gather and pray. Sometimes, they would go for many hours without eating. (This is called *fasting*.) They wanted to meet and pray to God even more than they wanted to eat. Other times, these people would stay up all night praying. Some of them would lie on the floor for hours, crying out to God. Yes, these could be *noisy* prayer meetings! As the people prayed, they asked God, "Please give us fifty souls this week—fifty new people who will believe in you." (Some weeks, they asked for 100 souls!) Usually, God answered their prayers, and then some! So many people came to hear about God that the meetings had to be held outside because Bradford had no buildings big enough to contain the crowds.

Smith grew to love prayer, just like the people in the Salvation Army did. He found that when he prayed before speaking to people, they were more likely to listen to what he had to say. Bit by bit, he was learning how God works.

GOD FAVORS HIM

Then God sent a special man to work in the mill with Smith. He was an older man who was very godly. He helped Smith grow even closer to God. And he taught Smith about baptism. Soon, Smith was baptized. This man also taught Smith the skills he needed to become a plumber. (He didn't want the boy to be stuck working long hours in a mill all his life.) By his 18th birthday, Smith was ready to put his plumbing skills to use. He put on his best clothes and went to see the head of a plumbing firm.

"Please," he asked, "can I have a job?"

"I ain't got no jobs going," the boss man said gruffly.

Smith was disappointed, but he thanked the man politely and turned to leave.

Before he walked out the door, the boss called after him. "Wait a minute, young man," he said. "You know, there is something different about you. I just cannot let you go."

So, the teenaged Smith Wigglesworth became a professional plumber. And wherever he worked, he talked about Jesus. He also did a brilliant job as a plumber. He could install pipes for a whole house in just a few days. In fact, Smith was too good at his job! He worked so quickly and skillfully that soon there were no more broken sinks or toilets for him to fix—and no new pipes that needed installing.

Smith was growing as a plumber, but, more importantly, he was growing as a Christian.

He was learning to pray in a way that pleased God. And he felt that God wanted him to tell more and more people about the gift of salvation. He had met some amazing people in the Salvation Army who had really helped him. One of this army's most amazing people was a pretty young woman named Polly.

CHAPTER 3

THE LADY FROM THE ARMY

Mary Jane (Polly)

POLLY MEETS JESUS

Mary Jane Featherstone (or Polly, as everyone called her) was brought up in a very strict home. Her parents were Christians whose lives revolved around God. Polly's parents taught her about God, but they also wanted her to learn a skill that she could turn into a job someday. So they sent her off to learn all about making hats. But after one month of hat-making, Polly said "Enough!" She didn't know what she wanted to do with her life, but she knew it did not include sewing hats!

Eventually, Polly moved to Bradford (where Smith lived) and began work as a servant in a house. One day, Polly was walking down a street when she saw a large crowd of people gathered in the marketplace. Polly edged toward the crowd for a closer look. She saw a band, playing and singing a lively song about Jesus. When the music stopped, a woman stood on a wooden box and started to talk about "salvation."

The crowd didn't seem to care much about this topic. Some of them started shouting at her. Then someone hurled a rotten egg. It smacked the lady right in the face. Stinky egg goo ran down her cheek, but she kept on preaching! Polly pushed her way to the front of the crowd. She had to get a closer look at this lady, preaching with rotten egg on her face. The woman begged the people, "Please, give your lives to Jesus." By this time in her life, Polly had met a few Christians. But no one like this!

The lady on the box announced, "We're going to the local theater to talk more about Jesus. Please join us!" Polly followed the group that headed toward the theater. When

Polly arrived at the theater doors, she paused. Her dad had always told her that theaters were "places full of sin." Polly did not want to sin. But then she thought about the lady on the wooden box. *That la•y was full of the love of Jesus,* Polly reasoned. *An• at this meeting, people are going to talk about Jesus. So it can't be a sin to go insi•e.*

Polly entered the theater and found a seat. She watched person after person climb up on the stage and tell the story of how God had saved them. When everyone's story had been told, the strange "egg lady" invited people to come forward and "give your life to Jesus." Polly felt her eyes fill with tears. Growing up, she had learned a lot about God, but she had never chosen to follow Him. She stood and moved to the front of the building. There, she knelt to pray. The preacher lady came over to her, and Polly said, "I want to give my life to Jesus." Polly prayed. When she finished, she felt like a huge weight had been lifted from her shoulders. She felt different inside. She leaped to her feet and shouted, "Hallelujah, it's done!"

SMITH MEETS POLLY

All the while, a young man was watching Polly. Smith Wigglesworth had come to the theater too. He had seen Polly enter. And he noticed her going forward, with tears in her eyes. When he heard her shout, Smith knew something: God was with this young woman.

Before long, Polly was helping others know Jesus the way she did. She joined the Salvation Army and quickly became an officer. She preached whenever she had the chance. Soon, Smith joined the Salvation Army too. Now, Polly and Smith were very different from one another—even though they were the same age. Polly came from a rich home. Smith's family was poor. Polly could speak fluently and powerfully, Smith stuttered whenever he tried to speak in public. Polly was well-educated. Smith still couldn't read. He had never learned.

However, Polly and Smith both loved Jesus. As they worked together, they became very good friends. In fact, they became such good friends that it looked like they were going to marry. But there was a big problem. According to the rules, a Salvation Army officer could *only* marry another officer. Polly was an officer. Smith wasn't. Then the Salvation Army decided to send Polly to one of its bases beyond Bradford. Some of the leaders didn't want Smith and Polly to marry—if Smith ever became an officer. (They were afraid that if Polly got married, she might leave the Salvation Army.) So they sent Polly to a base in Leith, Scotland, hundreds of miles north of Bradford.

Once Polly was gone, Smith realized he didn't want to live in Bradford anymore. He was now 20 years old, and he was a skilled plumber. *Well*, he thought. *I can work as a plumber anywhere.* So, he moved to Liverpool, England. He hoped that a change of city would help him not to miss Polly so much. He didn't know when he would see Polly again. But he knew they would always be friends, no matter how many miles separated them.

DARING DEEDS

Meanwhile, Polly was leading people in Scotland to believe in God, just as she had done in England. Polly was a bold young woman with a strong mind. She was determined to serve God, and nothing was going to stop her. Yes, she was far away from her good friend Smith, but she was still very close to her friend Jesus.

One of Polly's new friends in Scotland's Salvation Army was married to a man who did not want to have anything to do with God. He would shout at his wife and tell her to stop going to church meetings.

One day, Polly visited the lady in her home. After a while, they started to pray together. As they were praying, the husband came home from work. When he saw people praying in his home, he grew furious.

"Stop praying!" he ordered. "This is my home! You are not allowed to pray here." His wife was scared, but Polly kept on praying.

The man shouted at Polly, "If you don't stop praying, I will pick you up and throw you out of my house!" Polly kept on praying. The man rushed over to Polly and picked her up.

His wife begged him, "Please, put her down!"

What did Polly do? She kept praying. "Lord, save this man," she said.

Swearing loudly, the man started to carry Polly, who was *still* praying, down the stairs of his house. The man stopped at the top of the final flight of stairs. Polly feared that he was going to throw her the rest of the way down. Then she realized that the man was crying. He placed her down gently at the top of the stairs and knelt beside her.

"God can forgive you all of your sins," Polly told him. "All you have to do is ask." Then, right there on the stairs, Polly led the sobbing man to Jesus.

SMITH HELPS THE NEEDY

Back in Liverpool, Smith was striving to serve God too. He was working as a plumber, but his job was not the most important thing in his life. He spent much of his time thinking about all of the poor and desperate people living in Liverpool, especially the children.

As he walked around the city, he saw children who were so poor that they had almost no clothes to wear. They spent their days digging through garbage bins to find something to eat or drink. One time, he found a five-year-old boy who must have found an unfinished bottle of a strong drink called "liquor." The poor little boy was drunk. Smith knew that the alcohol could have killed him. So many children were living horrible lives and it broke Smith's heart. Smith could not stand to see children suffer. He remembered how hard his childhood had been and he decided to do something to help these kids.

So what did he do?

Every week, Smith spent almost all the money he earned to buy food for the hungry kids. When he had fed every kid in sight, he wandered through the streets, looking for more children to help. If he found kids with no place to live, he would invite them to his home. Once the kids had eaten, Smith told them how much Jesus loved them. For the first time in their lives, these children felt that somebody cared about them. Smith helped many of them believe in Jesus.

Smith spent every Sunday praying and fasting. He prayed that God would help him find and help more children. God answered these prayers. Every week, Smith would lead at least 50 young people to Jesus.

Next, Smith started visiting sick and wounded people in hospitals. He also went down to the docks and preached to sailors who were passing through Liverpool. Many of these "tough guy" sailors were so overcome by God's love that they cried. Dozens of the people Smith talked to decided to follow Jesus. The leader of Liverpool's Salvation Army base saw how much Smith loved people. Now, if you had met Smith Wigglesworth, your first impression would probably be, "This plumber guy looks tough. He is probably really mean." But Smith loved God, and he loved people. Because of this great love, the Liverpool Salvation Army leader thought Smith should speak in a church service. Smith wasn't sure how he felt about speaking in the church service; it made him nervous to think about it because he remembered how he would stutter when he spoke in front of crowds. Sometimes, he would begin a sentence, but become so tongue-tied that he couldn't finish it. And he still couldn't read. How could he preach from the Bible when he could recognize only a few of its words?

To make things even harder, Smith was so compassionate that when he spoke in church, he would look out into the audience and see so many who didn't know Jesus that it made him so sad that he would start to cry. He described himself as "a man with a fountain of tears." But even though speaking wasn't easy for Smith, when he preached, many people came to the front of the church to follow Jesus. Clearly, the power of God was with this young man.

Smith's friendship with Polly also helped him to keep on serving God. Smith and Polly were still very close friends, even though they lived far away from each other. Every week Polly would write to Smith. As Smith couldn't read the letters he had to ask a friend to read it for him. Then every week Smith's friend would help him write back to Polly.

In one of her letters, Polly told Smith that she was going to leave the Salvation Army and come back to Bradford. Smith had been away from Polly for three years. Now he wanted to be near her. So he decided to join her in Bradford.

The two friends were ready to start a great adventure together.

CHAPTER 4

THE FREEZE ATTACK

STARTING A FAMILY

Smith and Polly were not just *good* friends. They were best friends. They loved serving God together, and they loved each other. So, in 1882, they got married. They were both 23 years old.

During the first three years of their marriage, Polly patiently taught Smith how to read. He was so happy to learn. There was only one book Smith really wanted to learn about and now, at last, he could read the Bible for himself. Polly also taught her husband to write, but he never was very good at spelling.

Polly and Smith had five children: four boys and one girl. Their house was a busy place. In fact, things were busy everywhere. Smith and Polly weren't part of the Salvation Army anymore, but they were still part of "God's army." Wherever they went, they told people about Jesus. Many of these people decided to follow Jesus.

One of the neighborhoods in Bradford had no church. Smith was upset that the people in this part of town lacked a church they could call their own. Smith prayed about what he should do. He believed that God wanted him and Polly to start a church. Smith still didn't like preaching very much. Even though he had learned to read, he still struggled when he got up in front people to speak. His stuttering made it hard to get through just one sentence, let alone preach a whole sermon! Things were different for the well-educated Polly. Each Sunday, she would get up and preach from the Bible. Smith did his part by taking care of the church's children—including his own children. After Polly preached, she would ask her audience, "What would you like to do about what you have just heard?" That was Smith's cue. He would run to the front of the church. He couldn't preach a very good sermon, but he was awesome at helping people pray to Jesus, asking Him to be their friend and their guide for life. Smith and Polly made a great team and as Polly preached and shared God's Word from the Bible, Smith learned a lot about the Word of God from her.

As for Smith, his deep love for God was downright contagious. He was excited about God, and you couldn't be around him without becoming excited too. So the new church in Bradford grew and grew.

Meanwhile, Smith continued his work as a plumber. Because he was so skilled, he found himself in home after home and business after business, doing all kinds of plumbing.

God was blessing the Wigglesworths.

LOVE GROWS COLD

One winter, a blast of cold hit the whole city. People in Bradford couldn't remember when they had faced a winter storm as brutally cold as this one. Pipes froze and then cracked. (You probably know that water expands as it freezes into ice.) With broken and leaky pipes everywhere, it seemed like everyone needed a plumber. Smith had helpers, but not enough of them. He figured it would take him more than two years to fix all of Bradford's broken pipes! Because he was so busy, Smith started to miss a few church services. As time rolled by, Smith became so busy and so tired that he completely stopped going to church. Eventually, Polly was running the church by herself.

Meanwhile, all the work was making Smith grumpy—so grumpy that he didn't want to have anything to do with church or Jesus. Polly had her hands full running the church. But she knew she also needed to do something about her husband. Every day she prayed for Smith. The more she prayed, the closer she felt to Jesus. Polly was not only close to Jesus. She *behave*, like Jesus. She followed His example.

However, it was clear that Smith was NOT close to Jesus, as he had once been. In fact, it annoyed Smith that he and Polly had become so different. Because so many things were right about Polly's life, Smith had a constant, living reminder of how many things were *wrong* with his life!

Sometimes, Smith became so annoyed and angry with Polly that he actually shook with emotion. He sometimes shouted at her. But Polly just kept on loving her husband. The more he shouted at her, the more she showed love to him and prayed for him. Polly did her best to create a cheerful home. Deep inside, though, she longed to have her husband live for God again, and work side by side with her at the church. She often wondered to herself, *How could a man who was once so close to God be so far from Him now?* Polly would not give up on Smith. She knew God still had a plan for his life. She was careful not to nag Smith to go to church. That would just make him mad. But she tried to follow Jesus' example in the way she lived. And she kept praying and praying.

CHRIST IS MY MASTER

Polly served God in the church and beyond it. She roamed the city, leading hundreds of people to Jesus. She became a popular speaker. Other churches invited her to lead their meetings.

One time, Polly came home from church a little later than usual. Smith yelled at her: "I am the master of this house, and I am not going to have you coming home at so late an hour as this!" Polly replied calmly, "I know you are my husband, but Christ is my Master." Smith became furious. He grabbed Polly's arm and marched her out the back door. Then he slammed the door and locked her out. As he stared at the locked door, Smith started to feel guilty about what he had just done. "Why am I always so angry?" he asked himself. "Why am I so horrible to my wife? What has happened to my life?"

Meanwhile, Polly walked around the house and opened the front door. (Smith hadn't locked *that* door.) She laughed as she entered the house. Smith did his best to hold an angry expression. But Polly's laughter was contagious. Before long, both of them were laughing so hard that they were literally rolling on the floor laughing. As Smith lay there laughing with his wife, he realized that he needed to change. He had to stop running away from God. He had become a miserable person. He loved Polly, and he hated the way he was treating her. Smith wanted to change his life. He knew he needed to get close to God again, or he would never be happy. Smith decided to spend 10 days praying and going without food. As he fasted, he asked God, "Please, change my heart." Soon, Smith realized God was changing something inside of him. As the days went by, his anger faded away. He stopped complaining about the food Polly cooked for him. He became more like Jesus. Everybody he saw noticed the change.

God had answered Smith's prayers. And Polly's prayers. Now she and her husband could work together once more.

*Several sources cite Polly Featherstone's birth year as 1859. However, the month of her birth is unknown.

CHAPTER 5

THE FIRST TASTE OF MIRACLES

God's Servant

SHARING THE GOSPEL EVERY DAY

Smith was crazy about God again. He worked hard in the church, and he also talked about Jesus wherever he went. One day, while walking down a street, he prayed, "Show me the right man, God." The street was filled with people, but there was no one Smith felt he should approach. After an hour of looking, he felt frustrated. "Show me the right man, God," he prayed again. "But I don't have much time, so please hurry! After another half hour of waiting, Smith was ready to give up and go home.

Suddenly, a man rode past in a horse and cart. Immediately, Smith knew *this* was the one. He ran after the cart and started to tell the man about Jesus. The man stopped the cart. He looked at Smith and listened to him for a moment. Then he snapped, "Go away!" Smith was confused. He had waited so long for the "right" person to speak to, but this man clearly wasn't interested. On the other hand, Smith was sure God wanted him to talk with this man. So, Smith ignored the order to "Go away" and carried on talking about Jesus. Soon, the man started to cry. God's Spirit was changing this man from the inside—showing him that he needed to change his ways and ask forgiveness for the things he had done wrong. A few weeks later, Smith's mother approached him and asked,

"Smith, have you been telling someone about Jesus?"
"Always Mommy, why do you ask?"

"Last night, I went to see a man who was dying. When I asked him if he would like someone to pray for him, he told me that he hadn't left his house for three weeks. The last time he went out, someone told him about Jesus. At first, the man tried to ignore this person, but, eventually, he gave his life to Jesus. When the man described this 'someone,' it sounded very much like you." His mom added that the man had passed away that night. But he died knowing Jesus, thanks to Smith.

This episode was typical of Smith's life. He told non-Christians about Jesus. He prayed with Christians. Whenever he travelled, he visited local churches. He loved worshiping and talking with others who believed in God.

GOD CAN HEAL

One day, Smith went to Leeds to buy some pipes. While in Leeds, he attended a church meeting where sick people were prayed for. Smith watched, amazed, as people were healed. He was so excited to see God healing people that when he got home, he went into the streets and found some sick people. Then he paid for them to travel to Leeds so that someone in the church there would pray for their healing. Of course, lots of people laughed at Smith and those who believed God healed the sick and wounded. Even other Christians doubted that God would perform healing miracles, as He did back in Bible times. But Smith knew what he had seen. However, because he was afraid that people might laugh at him, he didn't tell Polly that he was sending people to Leeds.

Now, there were things Smith didn't understand about the church in Leeds. One time, he interrupted a healing service to ask the leaders, "If God can heal people, why do some of you have to wear glasses?" As you can see, Smith Wigglesworth was a straight-talking man who wasn't afraid to ask the kind of questions most people just wonder about. You never had to guess what he was thinking. Meanwhile, even though he had a few questions and doubts about healing, he brought people from Bradford to Leeds every week.

The leaders of the church thought it was really strange that Smith was bringing so many people to Leeds because he wanted God to heal them. He didn't seem to realize that God could heal them anywhere and all he had to do was pray for them. After a while, Polly found out what Smith was up to. She didn't think he was crazy. She listened with great interest when he told her all about the healings. In fact, Polly needed some healing herself. She was not feeling well. So she joined him on his next trip to Leeds. The leaders prayed for her, and she was instantly healed! Now, Smith and Polly knew that Jesus could save people's souls and heal their bodies as well. They knew that healings would become a part of their ministry.

GOD CAN HEAL ME!

Their church in Bradford continued to grow. Soon, the Smith and Polly realized they had to find a bigger building. A building on Bowland Street looked big enough to handle the crowds. Smith and Polly called it the Bowland Street Mission. In the building's entryway, they painted a picture of a scroll with the words "I Am the Lord that Healeth Thee."

When people came to the Bowland Street Mission, Polly and Smith taught them about God's healing power. They also prayed for the sick. Oddly enough, Smith was pretty sick himself. He suffered from a painful type of blisters called hemorrhoids, which appear on a person's backside and sometimes the blisters would bleed when he used the toilet. So, Smith took medicine for his problem.

One day, Bowland Street Mission featured a special guest preacher. After he preached, this man joined Polly and Smith for lunch. Polly wondered if the preacher could help her husband.

"Sir," she asked him, "what would you think if somebody prayed to heal the sick, but he took medicine for his own problem?"

The preacher replied, "I would think that person did not really believe God could heal him." Smith said, "She's talking about me." He explained his painful and embarrassing problem to the man, and they prayed together. Smith decided to stop taking any medicine. He knew that the bleeding would start again—unless God healed him. On the third day, he went into his bathroom. He anointed himself with oil. Then he asked God, "Do what You want to, quickly." The day ended, and there was no sign of the problem that had been bothering Smith. Day after day came and went, and the story was the same. Smith would live the rest of his life with no more hemorrhoids and the bleeding associated with them. God had healed him completely! Smith was so excited! He wanted to pray for anybody who was sick.

BUT I CAN'T PREACH

Smith was grateful to God that so many people were being healed of various problems. But he could not preach a sermon. Sunday after Sunday, Polly would announce to the Bowland church, "Smith will preach next week." But every time Smith tried, he could barely finish a sentence. He stumbled and fumbled his words. People could not understand what he was trying to say. Finally, Polly would have to stand up and take over for her husband.

Then the church in Leeds asked Smith to come and preach one Sunday. All of the leaders were going to a conference, so they needed Smith to do the sermon. Smith was not excited about it. He doubted that he was up to the task. Finally, he agreed to lead the singing and the prayers, but he insisted that somebody else was going to have to come to the pulpit to preach the sermon. When the time came for the sermon, no one came forward. Everyone in the congregation said that Smith should preach. He was left with no choice. Smith did his best to share a few words. Then he invited people to come forward if they wanted God to heal them. Fifteen people responded to his invitation. One man hobbled up on crutches. Smith prayed for him, and the man was instantly healed. He started to jump all over the place. The congregation was amazed. Smith was surprised too. He hadn't expected anything to happen, but people were actually being healed!

Smith decided to hold some healing services back in Bradford. On the first night, 12 people came forward. Every one of them was healed. One woman came forward with a large tumor. Smith prayed for her and sent her home. The next day, the tumor was gone. There was only a scar in its place! Smith knew God was using him in a special way. Many people invited Smith and Polly to their churches to pray for the sick. Others asked the couple to come to their homes. Wherever they went, God did amazing things.

CHAPTER 6

MORE AMAZING MIRACLES —AND A STAREDOWN WITH THE DEVIL

Praying for the healing

PRAYING FOR LIFE

Smith had a very close friend known as Mr. Clark. Mr. Clark's wife became very sick. Her health suffered so badly that doctors told Mr. Clark that his wife would not live to see one more day. This news left Mr. Clark sad and desperate. He wanted to believe that God could heal his wife, but he just couldn't do it. So he asked Smith to come and pray.

Smith loved his friend very much, and he didn't want his wife to die. God was giving him compassion. Smith made a decision: He was going to pray for Mrs. Clark, and God was going to heal her. Smith invited a fellow minister to visit the Clarks with him. The minister was happy to go along—until he heard that Mrs. Clark was about to die. Then he didn't want to come along anymore. So Smith called his friend Nichols. Nichols was known as a "big prayer." In other words, his prayers often went on and on, and sometimes people couldn't make sense of them. Nichols agreed to go with Smith to see the Clarks and even though Nichols had a bit of a strange reputation, Smith was happy to have someone with him when he entered the home. "You pray first," he told Nichols. "Pray for as long as you like. When you have finished, I'll pray." But as soon as Nichols started praying, Smith realized he should not have asked Nichols to pray. "Oh Lord, please look after this family as this lady dies," Nichols said. "Take care of them and comfort them." From there, Nichols's prayer went on and on and on. But he never once asked God to heal Mrs. Clark.

Smith was so frustrated over how things were going that he started to pray in a whisper, "Lord please *stop* this man from praying." But Nichols did not stop. Finally, Smith couldn't take it any longer. He shouted, "STOP!" Nichols stopped—right in the middle of a sentence. Then Smith invited Mr. Clark to pray for his wife. Unfortunately, the husband's prayer was the same as Nichols's prayer. Mr. Clark even said, "Lord, please answer my brother Nichols's prayer. Comfort me on this sad day, and prepare me to be able to get through it."

Smith could not believe his ears. Three men had joined together to pray for a woman's healing, but nobody had actually prayed for healing! "Lord," Smith shouted, "STOP HIM!" Smith's prayer was so loud that people out on the street could hear it! Mr. Clark stopped praying.

LET'S DO THIS PROPERLY

Smith yanked a bottle of oil out of his pocket. He poured the oil all over Mrs. Clark. Some of the oil spilled onto the bedding. Smith didn't care about the mess. As he poured oil, he cried out, "In the name of Jesus, may this woman be healed!" Then Smith put his hands on Mrs. Clark's head and kept praying, with boldness and passion. As he prayed, he looked toward the foot of the bed. There stood a vision of Jesus himself! Jesus was smiling gently at Smith. After a few moments, the vision disappeared. But Smith would remember it forever. What's more, Smith understood that Jesus had been waiting for someone to pray with faith and that's exactly what he had done. Mrs. Clark sat up, completely healed. Later, she would have children. In the end, she lived longer than her husband. Mrs. Clark's healing made Smith more determined than ever to live for Jesus. It would not matter what anybody else did or said. Smith decided that the Bible would be the only book allowed in his house. In fact, it would be the only reading material of any kind. No newspapers would be allowed, and no magazines.

"Jesus has given us everything we need in the Bible," Smith said. (If he were alive today, Smith wouldn't have even read *this book*—even though it includes stories of God's love and power.) Smith and Polly made another decision. They would never take any kind of medicine or see a doctor for any illness or injury. Instead, they said they would rely on "Doctor Jesus."

They did allow one exception to the rule. If Smith or Polly was about to die, a doctor would be called. But they didn't want the doctor to try to heal whoever was sick. They wanted the doctor to be a witness so that no one could say, "Smith begged Polly to let the doctor heal him, but she refused!" (Or vice versa.) It's important to realize that Smith and Polly didn't start out with such high levels of faith.

They had a passion to serve Jesus and live for Him. As their passion grew, they believed that God was leading them in a certain direction, and they were determined to follow it. Soon after the couple made their "Doctor Jesus" rule, they faced a big test.

POLLY, I'M DYING

One day, Smith felt a sudden stabbing pain in his stomach. In the months that followed, the mysterious pain came and went. Eventually, the pain got so bad that Smith could do little but lie in bed. He was sure he was dying.

"Polly, it looks like I am going to heaven," he said. "To protect yourself, you should call a doctor now, as we have planned." These words crushed Polly's heart. She went out to find a doctor. After the doctor examined Smith, he had bad news. Smith had appendicitis, and his appendicitis was so bad that not even surgery could save him. He was going to die. After delivering his grim verdict, the doctor left, with a promise to come back and check on Smith a bit later.

As the doctor left, an elderly woman and a young man came into the Wigglesworth house. This woman believed that all sicknesses came from the devil, and she announced that she and the man had come to pray for Smith. The young man got onto the bed and put both his hands on Smith.

"Come out, devil, in the name of Jesus!" he cried. Smith was very surprised when "the devil came out," and the pain disappeared. The couple prayed for Smith one more time. Then they left.

Smith got up, put his clothes on, and went downstairs. When he saw Polly, he smiled at her. "I am healed," he announced. "Any plumbing work for me to do?" Polly couldn't believe her eyes! The last time she had seen Smith, he appeared close to death. Now, only moments later, he was completely healed. She handed him a list of plumbing jobs that needed to be done. Smith left the house—with his plumbing tools, but *without* his appendicitis. When the doctor returned, he was shocked to find out that Smith had gone out to work. "That man has gone out," he predicted, "but his dead body will be the only thing that comes back." Years later, Smith liked to joke that his "dead body" was travelling all over the world and preaching the Gospel.

GOD'S WAY OR NO WAY

Meanwhile, Smith continued to learn more about the power of prayer. He knew what could happen when *everyone* in a room believed God could do a miracle. One evening at around 10 o'clock, Smith was called to pray for a young woman who was dying from tuberculosis, a devastating disease that attacks the lungs. Her doctor had given up on her. When Smith saw her, he understood why. This poor woman was in bad shape. Unless God did something amazing, she wouldn't live much longer. Smith turned to the young woman's mother. "Well, mother, you have to go off to bed now." The mother protested: "I have not changed my clothes for three weeks, because I have spent day and night next to my daughter. I'm not going to leave her now." Smith spoke to the sick woman's sisters: "You have to go to bed." Like their mother, the sisters refused to leave.

Then he spoke to the woman's brother: "You must go to bed." He refused too. "Okay, then," Smith said. "Good-bye. I'm off." He picked up his coat and walked out of the house. The family ran after him. "Please don't leave us," they begged. But Smith knew what he was doing. He knew that if the family members were hanging around, full of grief, it would be hard for him to pray for healing. He tried to explain the situation to them. "I can do nothing here," he said, "if you won't do the one simple thing I have asked of you." And so the family went off to bed, leaving Smith alone with the sick young woman.

JESUS CAN DO IMPOSSIBLE THINGS

As he knelt by the bed, Smith found himself face to face with death and the devil. From 11 p.m. until 3:30 a.m., he prayed for the young woman. Finally, the exhausted Smith saw the woman's life leaving her body. He kept praying, but soon the woman was still. She was dead.

This was not the result Smith expected. He felt the devil taunting him, "You are done for," came the hateful words. "This woman has died while you were alone with her." Smith was not ready to give up just yet. He had come to this house to pray for her, and he did not think that God had sent him for nothing. He remembered Jesus' words from Luke 18: "People should keep on praying and not give up." Smith was determined to keep praying, to keep trying.

He cried out to God again—with a new passion and strength. Suddenly, in the bedroom window, Jesus' face appeared. Light seemed to pour out from Jesus into the room. Jesus looked at the young woman and the color returned to her face. She rolled over and went to sleep. Smith knew he would *not* sleep, even though he had been up most of the night. He had seen God raise someone from the dead. Better still, he had seen Jesus again! He spent the rest of the night praising Jesus.

The next morning, the resurrected young woman woke up, put on her dressing gown, and began to play the piano and sing. As she made music, her brother, sisters, and mother rushed to see her. They were amazed. There she was, perfectly healed by Jesus.

God had used Smith to preach the Gospel, heal the sick, and even raise the dead. But, as hard as it might be to believe, God had even bigger plans.

CHAPTER 7

BAPTIZED IN THE HOLY SPIRIT

Anointing oil bottle used by Smith Wigglesworth

GOD'S DOING SOMETHING NEW

God had done so many amazing things through Polly and Smith, and they were sure they were, as some people call it, "baptized in the Holy Spirit." God was performing miracles through them, and He was helping to keep them away from sin. Life was very good.

But in 1907, when Smith was 48 years old, he heard news of something strange and wonderful happening in a church in Sunderland, England, a church led by a man named Alex Boddy. Mr. Boddy had seen amazing things happen in the country of Wales, as well as in the United States. And now similar things were happening in his own church.

The Sunderland newspapers began to report stories of people speaking in strange languages.

Smith had heard about this gift from God. He wanted anything that God was giving out. Some people from Bowland Street Mission had moved to Sunderland, so Smith decided to write them letters asking what was going on in their town. Some of these people wrote back to Smith. "Stay away from Alex Boddy and his church!" they warned. "He and his people have devils inside them. They are really strange." Despite the warnings, Smith decided he needed to investigate things for himself. He travelled to Sunderland and visited some of his friends. He prayed with them, and they encouraged him to follow God's leading. Then he went off to attend a meeting led by Alex Boddy.

WHERE IS THE FIRE?

Smith's head buzzed with excitement as he sat in the congregation, waiting for something spectacular to happen. After a while, his excitement faded away. The meeting was turning out to be boring. Back at his church, people would sometimes fall over when he prayed for them and they were filled with God's power. Back home, the praise music was lively, and it was easy to feel God's presence. Smith wasn't shy about sharing his opinion—even in the middle of a church service. So he announced, in a loud voice, "I have come from Bradford, and I want to have the experience of speaking in tongues—just like Jesus' followers experienced on the Day of Pentecost. Back in Bradford, our meetings are on fire. Yours don't seem to be."

A few people from Boddy's church led Smith outside. "You must not disturb the meeting," they told him. But he kept on asking questions. He was desperate to experience this "baptism in the Holy Spirit." He left the church and went to the local Salvation Army building to pray. As he prayed, he fell to the ground three times. The people in the building warned him not to speak in tongues, but Smith had read about it in the Bible, so he wanted it. He prayed for days, expecting that he would start to speak in tongues. A week went by. Nothing happened. Smith felt so discouraged. He decided it was time to return to Bradford.

YOU NEED TO BE BAPTIZED

On his way out of town, he stopped to say goodbye to Mary Boddy (the pastor's wife). "I'm so disappointed," he told her. "I really wanted to speak in tongues, but nothing has happened." "Mr. Wigglesworth," Mary replied, "it is not tongues that you need. You need to be baptized in the Holy Spirit." Smith asked her to pray for him. She agreed and offered a simple prayer. As she prayed, Smith felt the fire of God fall on him. He could feel the power of God inside him. He saw a vision of an empty Cross—and he saw Jesus seated next to God the Father. Overcome by this powerful experience, Smith opened his mouth to praise God. But the words he offered were not in English. They were from a strange language that he didn't know. He understood what was happening to him: He was speaking in tongues, just like Jesus' followers on the day of Pentecost.

Smith decided not to go home just yet. Instead he went straight to a meeting that Reverend Boddy was holding. Smith marched in and interrupted the service.

"I want to say something," he announced. Then he told everyone what had just happened to him. When he finished speaking, 50 people were baptized in the Holy Spirit. They started to speak in other languages too. The local newspaper wrote about what happened that day.

Smith sent a message home, sharing his story. He was so excited that he just had to announce it. At the same time, he wondered if some people back at his church might not be happy about what had happened to him. He was right.

GOD REALLY HAS DONE SOMETHING

When he returned, Polly met him at the front door. "I want you to know that I have been 'baptized in the Holy Spirit,' just as you were. I don't speak in tongues, but I don't believe I need to do that. On Sunday you are going to preach, with no help from me. That way, we will see if anything has *really* happened to you."

Polly knew that this was a huge challenge for her husband. Smith was still terrible at preaching. For years, she had tried to help him improve, but his sermons were always disasters.

Sunday came. Polly sat at the back of the church and watched her husband start to preach. She was amazed. Smith spoke with great power and real authority. He didn't stumble over any of his words. "That's not my Smith, Lord. That's not my Smith" she kept muttering to herself.

At the end of the service, a man stood. "I want to experience what you have," he told Smith.

As the man tried to sit, he missed his chair and fell to the floor, under God's power. Then Smith's oldest son stood up. "I want to experience what you have," he said. As he tried to sit, he fell over too. Before long, 11 people were on the floor, so overcome with God's power that they were laughing. God was pouring out his Holy Spirit on the whole congregation. Many people were speaking in other tongues. Before long, Polly joined in.

A NEW AUTHORITY FROM GOD

Word spread about what had happened at Smith's church. One evening, Smith came home from work and entered through the back door. "Which way did you come in?" Polly asked when she saw him. "Through the back. Why?" "Well, loads of neighbors are round the front. And there is an old man upstairs who is making so much noise that he has disturbed everybody. The man is 80 years old, and I think he's going crazy!"

Immediately, Smith heard the Holy Spirit whisper to him, "This is what I baptized you for." Smith went upstairs and opened the door slowly. Inside, the man was crying out. He was so upset. "I am lost! I am lost!" he cried. "God will never forgive me!" Somehow, Smith knew just what to do. "Come out, you lying spirit!" he commanded. Immediately, the evil spirit inside the man came out of him. The man calmed down. The house was peaceful again.

Before long, people everywhere wanted Smith and Polly to speak at their churches. Wherever they went, people were freed from sinful habits, healed from sickness, delivered from demons, and baptized in the Holy Spirit.

A HUGE LEAP OF FAITH

God's Student

FULL TIME FOR JESUS

The more Smith traveled, the more God used him. And the more God used him, the more he was asked to speak. Soon, Smith was travelling so much that he hardly had any time to work as a plumber. Because of Smith's busy schedule, his customers had to find other plumbers. This meant that even when Smith *was* home, there was no work for him. He and Polly knew they would have to trust God to provide the money they needed to survive.

After one long preaching trip, Smith came home to find that he had only one plumbing job on his schedule. He went to the home of a widow. He fixed a leaky pipe and repaired a ceiling that had been damaged by the water leaking on to it. The widow tried to pay Smith, but he refused to take the money. "I'm not going to take any money from you," he explained. "Instead, this job is going to be a special job for God. It is my last plumbing job . . . ever."

Smith closed down his business and went into full-time ministry. "As I'm doing this, God," he prayed, "I just ask You to make sure that my shoes don't wear out and my trousers don't have holes in them. If that happens I'm going to return to being a plumber—because I'm not going to have people saying that You can't provide for me. I won't have people thinking badly about You because of the clothes I wear." Smith remembered well the poverty of his childhood, and he didn't want his children to have an experience like his. But God looked after Smith's whole family. They always had food and clothing. Smith never had to go back to plumbing.

GOD IS WITH ME

Wherever Smith went, it was obvious that God was with him. In one town, he entered a shop and three people inside fell to their knees and asked God to forgive them for the sin in their life. Smith didn't even have to say a word! As he left the shop, Smith passed a field where two ladies were working—collecting some kind of a crop in buckets. He called to them, "Are you saved?" They dropped their buckets and called out to God to save them. Yes, God was using Smith in a new way.

Years earlier, some people from South Wales had visited the Bowland Street Mission. They had told Smith about a man called Lazarus who lived in the village and had been sick for a very long time. Smith had filed this story away in his memory. Now, Smith's travels brought him to South Wales—home to that man called Lazarus. As he prepared to minister in South Wales, Smith spent a day up a mountain, praying to God. As he prayed, he heard God speak to him: "Smith, I want you to go and raise up Lazarus."

So Smith went to the village and looked for people who believed God could heal Lazarus. But after much searching, he found only two people who believed such a miracle was possible. Of course, Smith knew the Bible story about another man named Lazarus, whom Jesus raised from the dead. When Smith saw the "South Wales Lazarus" and how sick he was, he knew God was going to have to perform another huge miracle. Lazarus was just a pile of flesh and bones, lying on a bed.

That night, Smith didn't eat anything. He spent dinner time praying instead. He went to bed, but when he woke up, he felt as ill as Lazarus looked. He cried out to God to heal him. God did heal him. Smith shouted out his thanks, but no one in the house where he was staying woke up. Then, at about 5 in the morning, God woke up Smith and told him to avoid eating anything until Lazarus was healed. God wanted Smith's next meal to be communion with Lazarus. Smith spent the next hour praying. Then he heard God say, "I will raise him up." Smith was thrilled to hear that Lazarus would be healed!

By 8 in the morning, everyone else in the house was awake. They offered Smith breakfast, but he knew God didn't want him to eat yet. Instead, he headed for Lazarus's house. Six people joined him.

LAZARUS IS CHANGED

In Lazarus's small bedroom, Smith spoke a few words that he hoped would build the man's faith. But Lazarus didn't seem to want this. Some people had prayed for him a few years ago, he told Smith, but nothing had changed. Smith and his companions stood in a circle, holding hands. Then Smith spoke: "We are not going to pray; we are just going to say the name of Jesus."

They all knelt together and began to whisper Jesus' name. Soon, God's power filled the room. It rushed in, and then moved away, like a mighty wave. This happened five times. But Lazarus was still sick. "This is what happened last time," Lazarus grumbled, "I'm never going to be healed." Smith replied, "I don't care what the devil says, and I don't care what happened last time. God has said that He will raise you up, so that is what is going to happen. Just think about Jesus—and only Jesus."

For a sixth time, God's power poured into the room. Lazarus' lips started to move. Then tears rolled down his cheeks. "I have been so bitter," he confessed. "I have upset God. It's not fair. I am sorry, God!" Those around the bed continued to whisper, "Jesus, Jesus, Jesus . . ." Suddenly, the bed shook. Lazarus shook, too, as God took hold of him. Smith sent his friends downstairs. Then he watched in amazement as Lazarus stood up, completely healed, and walked downstairs. People all over South Wales heard about what happened that day. Many of them decided to follow Jesus as a result.

SIMPLY OBEYING THE BIBLE

Even though he was becoming rather famous, Smith lived a simple life. He just wanted to follow Jesus. For him, faith meant truly trusting God to do what the Bible said He could do. Faith also meant that Smith Wigglesworth had to do what the Bible instructed him to do.

One day, Smith read Luke 14:13-14 in his Bible. These verses say that if you have a feast, you should invite the poor and needy. Smith thought this was a great idea. He and Polly made plans and got things ready for their feast. The couple wandered through the roughest parts of town and invited everybody to come and dine at Bowland Street Mission. On the day of the feast, Smith went to help a wheelchair bound woman get to the church. As he pushed her chair, one of its wheels fell off. Smith fixed the wheel, but soon it fell off again. He reattached the wheel again. "Don't worry too much about this old chair," he told the woman. "You won't need it much longer anyway."

On this day, Bowland Street Mission was filled with people. Many of them were homeless, so they could not bathe. Others were blind, led to the church by kind helpers. Still others wore bandages on various wounds—or coughed and coughed because they were very sick. The building didn't smell very good, even though there was lots of good food. Most people would not want to eat with these people, but Smith loved them. Many of those invited said, "This is the best meal I've ever eaten!" When everyone finished eating, Smith stood up. "Let's have some quiet, everyone," he announced. "It's time for the main event!"

As the diners looked on, some members of Smith's church came forward and shared how God had healed them of various diseases. Then Smith spoke again. "Today we have been telling you our stories of healing," he said, "but next week we are going to have another feast, and you are going to tell us *your* stories of how Jesus healed you!"

Then Smith called out in a loud, deep voice, "'Ooo wants to be 'ealed?" With that, he leaped off the platform and started to pray for people. It was absolute chaos. Some people jumped and shouted as God healed them. Others cried out, "God, save me!

One sickly boy was attached to an iron frame that supported his frail body. His mother tried to move him close to Smith, but there were too many people in the way. The mother thought for a moment. Then she passed her son overhead, from one person's hands to another. (If you have seen someone "crowd surf" at a football game, you get the idea.) When the boy reached the front of the church, he was laid at Smith's feet. Smith poured some oil on the boy's head and prayed for him to be healed. The boy cried out, "I can feel it going all over me. It's going all over me!" Then he rose to his feet. He was strong and healthy! Many people were healed that day, including the woman with the broken wheelchair. Another feast was held the following week. The poor and needy told how they had been healed, just as Smith had said they would. If you had been at either of these feasts, they would have reminded you of the miracles Jesus performed.

It seemed like nothing could stop Smith's ministry. But could something slow it down?

"PAIN, SO MUCH PAIN!"

Still preaching, no matter what

SOMETHING'S THE MATTER WITH POLLY

Smith continued to travel more and more. God opened doors to many places for him. One day, Smith was preparing for a train trip to Scotland. He heard a knock at his door. There stood a policeman. "I have news," the officer said, "and it is not good." "What is it?" Smith asked. "Polly has collapsed after preaching at the Bowland Street Mission," the officer said sadly. "She has had a heart attack and died." The news stunned Smith.

Polly's body was carried home. People told Smith how sorry they were, but he wasn't really listening. He had a plan. By this time in his ministry, Smith had seen several people raised from the dead. He knew God could raise up Polly too.

He requested that Polly's body be carried up to the bedroom. Then he excused everyone from the room and closed the door. Smith rebuked the spirit of death from Polly. Immediately, she opened her eyes. She was alive again! You might think that the couple would throw a huge party to celebrate. That didn't happen. Instead, Polly and Smith talked for a long time. Then Polly told her husband. "I have done everything God has told me to do on Earth. My work here is done, Smith."

Then Smith heard God speak to him, "This is the time that I want to take Polly home to be with me." Smith loved his wife so much. She had been his partner in ministry for decades. They had done everything together. Polly had taught him how to read. She was the mother of his children, and they were best friends. But Polly's time to go to Heaven had come. Smith's heart was breaking, but he knew he had to let her go.

On that day, January 1, 1913, Polly went home to be with Jesus. She was only 53 years old. Smith cried and cried. In fact, his heart hurt so bad that he asked God to take him to Heaven too. *Life without Polly will be no life at all*, he thought.

GIVE ME A DOUBLE ANOINTING

But as Smith knelt, crying and praying, God spoke clearly to him: "Get up, and walk away." As Smith left the room, he prayed, "Lord if you will not take me to heaven now, then give me a double anointing. Give me Polly's anointing, as well as my own. If you do that, I will go wherever you tell me to and preach the Gospel." God did increase Smith's anointing, but the days of sadness were not over.

The Wigglesworth children were grown up now, so Smith had to learn to live alone. Sometimes, he became so lonely that his body actually hurt. When he traveled for his ministry, he missed having Polly next to him. She was always so cheerful, always encouraging, and always focused on Jesus.

TWO YEARS LATER

About two years later, tragedy struck again. On March 22, 1915, Smith received the news that his youngest son,

George, had been killed in battle in World War I. Smith was crushed by the news. Yes, he drew some comfort from his other children, including his daughter, Alice, who had volunteered to help take care of him after Polly's death. Who could blame Smith if he decided, after all that had happened to him, to give up his ministry? But Smith knew he could not give up. For most of his life, he had encouraged people to trust God no matter what. Now he understood that he would have to follow his own teaching. He would have to cling to God just to cope with each day. Losing two beloved members of his family was the worst thing that had ever happened to Smith. He had thought his childhood was a hard time. It was nothing compared to *this*. He felt so alone.

However, something good came of Smith's suffering. When he saw other people dealing with pain and sadness in their lives, he felt even more love and compassion for them. He understood what they were going through. Yes, Smith found that he loved people more than ever. He also hated the devil and the evil he brought into people's lives. He was determined to share the good news of what Jesus had accomplished when he died on the Cross.

Because God had given Smith the "double anointing" he had prayed for, it was now time for him to make good on his promise to travel anywhere to preach the Gospel. Polly's part of this mission had been accomplished, but Smith still needed to finish his part.

CHAPTER 10

OFF TO AMERICA

Growing older

GEORGE, GOD IS CALLING ME

Soon after Polly's death, but before George had died, God told Smith to go to America.

One Sunday morning, Smith told his church that he would be crossing an ocean to minister on another continent. Everyone was shocked. They had already lost Polly. Now they were losing Smith too? When Smith saw the church's reaction, he knew he should make sure that God was truly leading him to a destination so far away. "Lord," he prayed, "you need to give me three things if you want me to go to America. I need money for a home there. I need money to travel across the ocean. And, I need you to improve my memory, because I keep forgetting things. This makes it hard for me to preach. For that matter, it makes it hard just to manage my life." Before long, money seemed to pour in from all over the place. This helped Smith know he was making the right decision.

But not everyone was so sure. Smith's son George was really sad. His mom had died. And now his dad was going away. George couldn't believe that this was what God wanted. So George sat down with his father and asked him to stay in Bradford. While the two men talked, someone knocked on the door. Smith told George to go and open the door. George obeyed and greeted a man who was holding a letter. "Open the letter," Smith told his son. Inside, he found 25 pounds—a lot of money back in that day.

George looked at the postmark on the envelope. He realized that it had been mailed six weeks previously—before Smith had even announced his decision to travel to America! As George thought about this, he realized that God did indeed want his father to make the trip.

Smith now had all the money he needed, but there was still the matter of his faulty memory. A few days later, a stranger approached Smith and, for no apparent reason, handed him a blank diary. As Smith flipped through the diary's blank pages, he got a clear message from God: "Use this book to write down everything that happens to you."

Smith obeyed. He immediately started using the book to record each day's events. To his amazement, he found that writing things down helped him remember *everything!*

And so God answered all of Smith's requests. On April 19, 1914, about a year after Polly's death, Smith set sail for North America.

SHARING THE GOSPEL ON BOARD

He didn't intend to wait until the ship landed to start preaching. He wandered around the ship, announcing, "I'm going to preach on Sunday. Do you want to come?" Unfortunately, not a single passenger seemed interested.

A few days later, some of the ship's crew approached Smith. "We're going to be holding some entertainment on board," one of them said, "and we want the passengers to come. Would you like to participate?" After praying about this request, Smith felt God's Holy Spirit calling him to use the show as an opportunity to tell people about Jesus. He went to the ship's staff and announced, "I will sing a song at the show, but I want to perform at the end of the program, just before the final dance."

The show featured all kinds of entertainment, including musical numbers. There was a lady playing the piano, but when the time came for Smith's song, she refused to accompany him. Apparently, she did not approve of his song choice. He sang anyway, without a piano. Smith sang a hymn from church. As he sang, people in the audience began to cry out and beg God to forgive their sins. By the time Smith finished singing, no one felt like dancing. Many of them came forward to devote their lives to Jesus. During the rest of the journey, many passengers talked with Smith about God. Finally, the ship landed in America. Smith got busy right away, planning and leading services.

CAN YOU HEAL ME?

In Cazadero, California, Smith got up to preach. A man who was almost completely deaf moved his chair right up to Smith's feet. Smith tried to heal the man. Nothing happened. Smith could sense the devil trying to discourage him by saying, "You're done for now. People are going to think you can't heal anyone!" But Smith did not give up that easily. He told the devil, "No, I am not done for. Jesus said, 'It is finished.' When He died on the Cross, He defeated sickness and death, once and for all."

For the next three weeks the deaf man attended Smith's meetings, always moving his chair right up front. But the man remained deaf, and the devil continued to mock Smith. Smith, meanwhile, kept right on reminding the devil what Jesus had accomplished.

After another week went by, Smith held another service. Everyone was worshipping God, but Smith noticed that the deaf man's face was a mask of worry. Then the man started to look all around him, in a panic.

Smith was very concerned. *Has this man gone crazy?* he wondered. Then the man leaped to his feet and sprinted out of the building. But he stopped when he got outside, because he heard a voice. It was God, telling him, "Your ears are now open." The man stood very still for a moment, and then he realized something. He could hear the song of worship from inside the building he had just left! The once-deaf man returned. As soon as he stepped in the door, the singing stopped. The man explained to the congregation that he had heard a loud noise—the only kind of noise he *coul* hear.

"I was afraid that the noise was an earthquake or something," he explained. "That is why I jumped up and ran away. I was trying to get to safety. But then I realized that

God had opened my ears, and I could hear!" Everyone went wild, praising Jesus. Smith joined in the praise. When Jesus had said, "It is finished," He really meant it.

SICKNESS FLEES

Sometime later, Smith held a service in Victoria, Canada. One of the people who came was a woman with breast cancer. Smith anointed her with oil and cast out the demon of cancer. The lady knew that she had been healed. Over the next few days, she felt the cancer leaving her body. Then, one day, the cancerous tumor dropped away, much like a scab.

The tumor left a crater about the size of a fist in the woman's skin, but in several days, healthy skin grew back. Before long, the crater had been filled. The woman placed the tumor in a glass jar, and brought it to one of the services so that she could show it to everyone. The people were excited. God had performed a miracle.

At a meeting in San Francisco, California, Smith met a 95-year-old man suffering from stomach cancer. The poor man had battled his painful disease for three years, and things were getting worse. For the past several weeks, he had been forced to survive on a liquid diet. He was too sick to eat any solid foods. Now, back in the early 1900s, few people lived to be 95, even if they were healthy. So almost no one held much hope for a 95-year-old man with cancer. "This must be his time to go," some of them reasoned.

Smith disagreed. He believed that the devil had caused this man's cancer. It had nothing to do with his age. Smith prayed for the old man, and he was instantly healed. Soon, he was telling people that he was free of pain and that he could eat solid food again. As he spoke, his whole face seemed to shine.

God did amazing things through Smith Wigglesworth. People crowded into buildings to hear him preach. People chose to follow Jesus. People were healed from all kinds of illness. There was no doubt in Smith's mind: God had truly given him the double anointing he had prayed for.

GOD CAN SET YOU FREE

In February of 1915, Smith knew it was time return to England. As his ship sailed back across the ocean, Smith sat near a man who was drinking whiskey. The man offered Smith a drink, but Smith told him, "I never touch the stuff." The man laughed, "How can you live without it?" he said. Smith replied, "How can you live *with* it? Just say the word and you will be delivered from the need to drink alcohol."

The man was confused. What in the world did Smith mean? Smith told him again, "Just say the word and you will be delivered." But the man didn't respond. Then Smith told the man to stand very still. He cast out the demon of alcoholism from the man. Immediately the man started shouting, "I'm free, I'm free." He threw away his whiskey bottles. Before the ship docked in England, the man chose to follow Jesus, and he was filled with God's Holy Spirit.

Smith realized that God was using him wherever he went—not just in church. Smith loved to help people know God better, whether he was preaching to thousands or having a private chat with just one man or woman. He just wanted to serve God, wherever and whenever. Smith loved God, and he loved people. God used that love to accomplish wonderful things.

CHAPTER 11

MIRACLES AND COMPASSION

Smith and daughter Alice

JESUS LOVES YOU
(EVEN IF YOU DON'T BELIEVE IN HIM)

Smith's worldwide travels taught him something: People everywhere needed Jesus.

For example, one day in a shop, Smith saw a man whose eyes were red and sore. He could tell the man was really suffering. As they began to talk, the red-eyed man told Smith, "My eyes hurt so bad that I can't even sleep." Smith placed his hands on the man's eyes and asked God to heal them. When Smith finished praying, the man looked at him. "This is so strange," he said. "I have no pain. I am free!"

A little while later, Smith visited the house of a man with cancer. The man was taking morphine (a very strong painkiller) every ten minutes, but he was still in agony. "Do you believe in God?" Smith asked the man. "No," came the reply. "I don't believe in God—and I don't want to believe!" Smith knew this man didn't really know or understand God. Otherwise, he wouldn't reject Him. Smith asked God to heal the man anyway. Within moments, the man's pain vanished. This encounter with God's power completely changed the man. Before he would talk non-stop about yachts. He was a member of an exclusive yacht club, and these expensive sea vessels were about the only thing he wanted to talk about. But after he was healed of cancer, all he wanted to talk about was Jesus.

DO I HAVE TO CHANGE?

Smith cared deeply about people, and he did not demand that they change their ways before he would introduce them to God or ask God to heal them. He knew that once people met God, they couldn't help but change! What's more, Smith loved people no matter what disease they suffered from, or what bad things they had done.

Once, a woman approached Smith. "I believe in God, but I also smoke cigarettes," she informed him. "What shall I do?"

"Carry on smoking night and day, if you want." Smith replied.

"I have a glass of wine now and then," she added. "Sometimes, I just have to have one."

"Keep on drinking, if you want," Smith replied.

"I like gambling and playing cards," she continued.

"Keep on playing, if you want," Smith replied again.

What, exactly, was he getting at? Didn't he want this woman to stop drinking, smoking, and gambling? Of course he wanted her to change. But he knew that she couldn't (or wouldn't) stop doing these things just because Smith Wigglesworth told her to.

He also knew that she couldn't break these habits by her own willpower. If this woman kept following God, however, Smith knew that, eventually, she would not want to smoke, drink, or gamble anymore. She would be able to stop, because God would change her heart. And that is exactly what happened.

You see, when we get to know God, He changes us. But if we try to change without meeting with God, we are trapped in a life of misery. Sometimes, a church or a religious leader might try to make you follow a long list of rules to make you "acceptable" to God. But the main thing God wants is simply for us to love Him. When we do that, He helps us live for Him and do the right thing.

That's why Smith was willing—and happy—to see God work in people's lives. He knew it was God doing the work, not Smith Wigglesworth or anyone else. For this reason, Smith didn't require someone to be a Christian for years before he or she could stand up in church and say, "This is what God has done for me . . ." Smith didn't demand that people be skilled speakers. He just wanted them to share their excitement about Jesus, any way they could. He knew that this would help others be excited about Jesus too.

GOD CARES ABOUT YOUR MIND

One day, Smith visited a lady who was mad. Right away, Smith could tell that a demon had made her crazy. Smith asked the family what they had done to help the woman.

"Oh, we've done everything possible to help her," the woman's sister replied. "What about spiritual help?" Smith asked. This made the woman's husband furious. "My wife carries on, acting crazy, day and night. Do you think we would believe in God after seven weeks of no sleep? If you do, you are in the wrong house!" At that moment, a young lady got up and walked out of the house. As this stranger left, she gave Smith a mean-spirited grin. She seemed to know that he could not help the poor woman.

Smith knew why the mysterious young lady had grinned at him. She was right. His own faith was not strong enough for this situation. However, he didn't have to depend on his faith. It was God's faith that mattered. Smith prayed for the "mad" woman.

As he prayed, he felt God's faith and power pour into his heart. He knew God was going to heal the woman. He turned to her, and called out to the demon inside her, "Come out of her, in the name of Jesus!" After Smith uttered these words, the lady fell asleep for 14 hours. When she woke up, she was perfectly well.

Wherever Smith went, he knew God had a purpose for him.

PLEASE PRAY FOR MY HUSBAND

One day, he stopped in to visit one of his friends, who was a spiritual leader in his church. The friend wasn't home, but his wife was. "God has sent you here to help me," the wife told Smith. "Let me tell you my story: God filled me with his Holy Spirit. But the leaders in my church, including my own husband, do not think that the Holy Spirit heals people or casts out demons or does other things that happened back in Bible times. In fact, my husband isn't allowed to be a church leader anymore—and it's all because of my beliefs about the Holy Spirit and how He can work through people today! I just can't quit talking about it." She continued, "When my husband was removed from leadership, he came home so angry with me. He blamed me for everything. He walked out of the house and said he was never coming back! Please, will you pray for him?"

"We need to pray that your husband comes back tonight," Smith told her. "Will you pray for this with me?" "He won't be back tonight," the woman replied. "I know he won't."

"He will be back if we agree in prayer together." The woman considered Smith's words. Then she agreed to pray with him. As they prayed together, the woman was filled with the Holy Spirit. "Your husband will be back tonight," Smith said. "When he comes home, show him lots of love.

But if he won't listen to you, just let him go off to bed." That evening, the woman's husband did come home. However, he refused to listen to anything she had to say. When he went to bed, his wife stayed up to pray for him.

She prayed for a long time. Finally, in the middle of the night, she sensed that her prayers had been answered. She went up to her sleeping husband, placed her hands on him, and said one more prayer for him. He woke up with a shout. Then he cried out to God, "Please have mercy on me!" That night, he was filled with the Holy Spirit, just like his wife.

GOD SAVES AND GOD HEALS

On another night, Smith visited the home of an elderly woman who had broken her leg in two places. She had worn a cast for several months, but her leg refused to heal. Her doctors weren't sure what else they could do to help her. Smith spoke to her gently, "Do you believe that God can heal you now?" he asked. "Only God can heal me. Yes, I do believe," she said. Her husband, however, didn't believe. He had been stuck in a wheelchair for four years, unable to walk. He called out to Smith, "I don't believe. I won't believe. You will never get me to believe!" Smith ignored him and prayed for the woman.

Then, with his help, she stood up. Her leg was completely healed! Her husband was shocked. "Make me walk! Make me walk!" he pleaded. Smith answered, "You old sinner, repent!" The man repented. As he did, the power came into his legs. He stood and walked. As you might guess, when people heard of miracles like this, they flocked to hear Smith preach the Gospel.

He also visited many places where people had never heard of him, but he didn't remain unknown very long. Wherever he went, he carried the presence of Jesus with him. He was always ready to do whatever Jesus told him to do.

CHAPTER 12

SMITH'S STRANGE ACTIONS

Unique ministry

DO IT!

When Jesus ministered on Earth, He reminded people that He did only what God, His Father, told Him to do. Smith tried to live that same way. In doing so, he found God telling him to do some strange things. Sometimes, for example,

Smith would start a meeting with a promise: "The first person in this audience who stands up, whatever his or her sickness, I'll pray for you, and God will heal you!"

Once, a man whose legs were badly twisted struggled to his feet—with the help of two walking sticks. Smith prayed for the man. He requested that everyone else pray too. Then Smith told the man, "Put down those sticks." The man obeyed. He tried to walk, but all he could do was shuffle along. "Walk!" Smith ordered. The man walked. Then, when Smith shouted for him to run, he started running. He was healed!

YOU KILLED HIM!

One Sunday afternoon, a man came to a service on a hospital trolley, accompanied by his doctor. "This man has cancer," the doctor explained. "He's dying." "Where's the cancer?" Smith asked. "In his stomach."

Smith made a fist and hammered it into the sick man's stomach as hard as he could. But the man was not healed. He died. "You've killed him! You've killed him!" the panicked doctor cried out. "His family will sue you!"

Smith looked at the dead body and said confidently, "He's healed." Then he walked away and prayed for the next sick person in the line. Ten minutes later, the dead man came back to life! He started to walk toward Smith, his hands lifted in praise. "I've been healed; I've been healed!" he cried out. Smith didn't even turn back to look at the man.

"Just praise God for it," he said. Then he carried on praying for others in the congregation.

OBEYING THE HOLY SPIRIT

As we have seen, Smith didn't have one set way of ministering to people. He didn't follow a formula. Sometimes he would anoint the sick with oil, as the Bible instructs in James 5:14. Other times, he would actually slap people or even punch them—as he did to the man with stomach cancer. He did this when he believed a demon had caused a disease. Each time he just listened to God and did what God told him to do. Lots of people criticized Smith's way of ministering. However, other people wanted to copy what he did and Smith knew that would be wrong, so Smith warned them not to. "Don't do what I do," he said. "Do what the Holy Spirit tells you to do!"

To the people who criticized him, Smith explained, "I'm just obeying God. If you are afraid to be touched, don't come to me and ask me to pray for you. But if you believe God can use me, then come to me and I will help you." Sometimes Smith would pray over a handkerchief which would then be taken to a sick person and when that person touched the handkerchief—or even got near it—he or she would be healed.

IS THIS POISON?

When Smith was ministering in the English city of Liverpool, a lady approached him. "Please, can you pray with me?" she pleaded. "My husband is a drunk. Can you pray with me that he will stop drinking alcohol?" "Have you got a handkerchief that I can use?" Smith asked. The lady gave him a handkerchief. Smith prayed over it. "Now take this handkerchief," he instructed, "and put it under his pillow." The woman followed the instructions.

That night, her husband came home drunk. He collapsed on his bed. He didn't know about the handkerchief under his pillow. In the morning, the man woke up and headed for work. As usual, he stopped at a pub for a beer. He took one sip of his drink. Then he yelled at the bartender. "You've put poison in this beer!" he accused.

The bartender denied it, so the man went to another pub and ordered a beer. This beer tasted weird too. He went to a third pub, with the same result. He was sure that all three pubs had tried to serve him poisoned beer! So, the man went to work without his customary beer. After work, he thought he would try again. Another pub, another strange-tasting beer! The man got very upset and he made such a fuss over his "poisoned drink" that he had to be tossed out of the pub!

When he got home, he complained to his wife, "Everyone has tried to poison me today," he explained. "I haven't been able to have a single drink!" "Can't you see what God is doing?" his wife said. "He is making you hate the stuff that has ruined your life." The words his wife spoke opened his eyes and his heart to the truth and that night he went to the church meeting and got saved.

WHAT'S YOUR SECRET?

People were so amazed at the way God used Smith. They wanted to know how he did it. They wanted to find out the "secret" of his faith.

Once, a woman asked him, "How long do you pray each day?" (She thought that if she prayed as long as Smith did, she might be able to perform miracles too.) "Madame," Smith replied, "I never pray for more than half an hour." This answer pleased the lady. She also prayed for about half an hour a day. Maybe she would start seeing miracles happen too? Then Smith interrupted her thoughts. "But," he told her, "I never go for more than half an hour without praying." Indeed, anyone close to Smith noticed that he never went very long without praying. After a meal, he always led his fellow diners in prayer. When visitors came to his house, they would spend only a short time visiting but a long time praying!

When Smith traveled by train, he spent most of the trip talking with Jesus. Of course, he didn't pray for the whole trip. Sometimes he stopped praying . . . to read his Bible! Smith believed in the power of prayer. He also believed in the power of faith.

One day, he was asked to visit the home of a woman who was dying. The moment he walked in the door, he heard her announcing, "I have faith! I have faith! I have faith!" She said the three words over and over, as if they were a magic spell. Smith could tell that she didn't truly believe what she was saying. "You don't have faith," he informed her. "You are just spouting words. You are dying and you know it." Then he asked her, "Do you want to be healed?" "Yes," she confessed sadly, "but I have no power." Smith prayed for her. Instantly, she returned to full health. Smith understood that merely saying you have faith is not enough. He believed that real faith leads to actions. "You don't do something to make something happen," he liked to say. "You do something because you know it is going to happen."

DECISION TIME

One time, Smith visited another person who was dying. This time, it was a man whose intestines had burst open inside of him. Infection had spread throughout his body, and he was covered with ugly open sores. It seemed there was no hope for this poor man.

His local doctors could not help him, so they had asked a specialist from the big city of London to try to help. While everyone was waiting for the specialist's arrival, Smith anointed the man with oil and prayed for him to be healed. At first, it looked like nothing had happened. Smith left the room where the man was lying, asking the others in the room to pray. Then the specialist arrived from London.

"The specialist is going to operate on my husband," the man's wife informed Smith. "No," Smith told her firmly. "You must not let him operate. If he operates, your husband will die. If there is no operation, he will live." (Smith knew that God had begun healing the man. It was just a matter of time until the healing process was finished.) The woman thought about Smith's words. Then she sent the specialist and the other doctors away. "I believe that if you operate on my husband, he will die," she informed them. "But if you don't, he will live." As soon as she spoke those words, her husband leaped out of bed, completely well. The specialist and the other doctors could not believe it. Every sore on his skin had vanished.

Once again, Smith had followed what the Holy Spirit told him to do, and whenever Smith did this, God did His part. For example, Smith visited a very sick woman, and he could tell immediately that she didn't have long to live. "What shall I do?" Smith asked God's Holy Spirit. "Read Isaiah chapter 53," the Holy Spirit instructed him. So Smith began to read this Old Testament Scripture aloud. When he reached verse 5, the woman leaped out of bed. "I am healed!" she shouted. "I am healed!" Notice that Smith didn't even pray for this woman. He just followed the Spirit's leading, and God did the healing. Miracles happened because Smith had obedient faith. He did what God told him to do.

GOD HAS NEVER SENT ME ANYWHERE TOO LATE

Another time, he visited a dying boy, whose parents told Smith, "It's too late. Our son is beyond help." Smith replied, "God has never sent me anywhere too late. Leave me alone with the boy." Fifteen minutes later that boy was up and out of bed and feeling fine. In fact, God's power filled the whole house that day. The boy's sister—who had apparently become mentally ill—was healed too!

Then there was the time Smith encountered a 9-year old boy who was very sick and weak. He had no appetite at all. Now, the boy's doctors thought that problem was "all in his head." They doubted that there was anything truly wrong with him. He just needed to start eating again and he would be fine.

God showed Smith that the boy's problem was in his stomach. The boy's mother disagreed with Smith. "They have X-rayed our son," she pointed out. "If there was something wrong with his stomach, it would have shown up on the X-ray." "Doctor Jesus knows better than your doctors," Smith declared. Then he placed a hand on the boy's stomach and prayed. The boy vomited—and out popped a 13-inch-long worm! The worm had been making the boy sick. Somehow the doctors had missed seeing it.

As we have seen, Smith based his whole ministry on reading the Bible and obeying God. Once, a lady came up to him and asked him if he had written a tract or a book about healing. Smith handed her his Bible. He told her, "The Gospels of Matthew, Mark, Luke, and John are the best tracts on healing that you will ever find. Read them and believe them. Then you will see God do amazing things." That is how Smith Wigglesworth lived his life. He followed the Bible—you and I can do the same thing too.

Of course, when you faithfully obey God's teaching, you are going to make some enemies. Jesus told His disciples this, and it is still true today.

CHAPTER 13

SMITH'S ENEMIES ATTACK

Smith ready for action

YOU DROP HER, GOD WILL PICK HER UP

"I want the person who is the most sick to come forward," Smith challenged one of his audiences. A few moments passed. Then a pale, sickly woman shuffled toward Smith. She needed two friends to help her.

"What's wrong?" he asked the woman. She whispered her reply. Smith nodded, and then told the whole congregation, in his booming voice, "This woman has cancer!"

He instructed the woman's friends, who were now holding her upright, "Let her go." The friends obeyed. The woman collapsed with a thud to the hardwood floor. Her legs were too weak to support her weight.

"Lift her up again," he ordered.

The ladies struggled, but they eventually helped their friend back to her feet. "Now let go," Smith said. The ladies hesitated.

They didn't want to drop their friend again, but they also didn't want to disobey this powerful preacher. So they did as they were told. Another collapse. Another loud thud.

The whole crowd gasped in horror and thought Smith wasn't healing this poor woman. He was hurting her! One man had seen enough.

He stood up and shouted, "Leave this woman alone, you brute!" "Mind your own business," Smith replied, "I know my business." Meanwhile, the friends had picked up the sick woman again. "Let go of her!" Smith boomed. The ladies hesitated.

"DO AS I SAY!" came the command. The crowd cringed, fearing another painful fall, as the women let go of her. This time, the woman stood. She swayed a bit, like a tree in the wind. Then a brown-gray lump fell from somewhere on her body and plopped onto the hard floor. The lump was a cancerous tumor. The woman was healed.

As we have seen, sometimes Smith's healing methods were unusual. And some people tried to sue him for hurting them in the process of healing them! However, none of the lawsuits were successful. Yes, Smith was sometimes rough with people, but he never really hurt anyone.

IT'S GOD'S MONEY

Other people questioned Smith's lifestyle, especially the way he spent his money. He was always well-dressed, in expensive-looking clothes. "What a waste of money!" some of his critics said. But Smith didn't see it that way. "I want to look good at all times," he explained, "because I am representing God. I don't want people to think that God can't provide for me."

Along with the fancy clothes, Smith insisted on traveling first class. On any train, you would find him in the "Luxury Carriage." "How can you waste God's money like that?"

people would ask him, accusingly. "I'm not wasting God's money," Smith would reply. "I am saving God's servant. I have to travel many miles all the time. I need to make sure I get a good rest. If I am going to have the energy and good health to minister, that's why I travel in comfort."

Now, it is important to understand that Smith looked for ways to stretch every penny—and to avoid living like someone who had lots of money. As a dinner guest, he would sometimes refuse to eat a meal if he felt too much money had been spent on it. Also, Smith did not go from place to place begging for money. He believed that God would provide for his needs, and he gave a lot of thought to how he spent money.

LIFE IN A PRISON CELL

Unfortunately, the questions about money were only the beginning of Smith's troubles. He sometimes got into trouble with the police—even though he strived to be a law-abiding citizen. While he was ministering in Switzerland, he was thrown in prison two different times. You see, because Smith healed people, the police accused him of practicing medicine without a license. That was against the law. During one of these times he was in prison a police officer came to

Smith's cell in the middle of the night to tell him that after considering things, the police had decided to set him free. However, Smith refused to leave his cell. "I cannot leave yet," he explained to the officer, "I haven't finished praying for every single police officer in the building."

Another time, the Swiss police came to a house where Smith was staying during a time of ministry. They planned to arrest him again. "I'm sorry," the person who owned the house told the police, "but Smith isn't here right now. He is leading a meeting a couple miles away. However, before you go to arrest him, I'd like to show you something." The person led the police to a nearby house.

The police knew all about this particular house. The lady who lived there was constantly in and out of prison. She liked to get drunk and cause trouble. However, when the police knocked on her door, they found the woman quite sober and in a very pleasant mood. "I went to a meeting with that evangelist Smith Wigglesworth," she told them. "He prayed for me, and I haven't drunk any alcohol since then." The police were dumbfounded. God had obviously done something amazing. They left and never tried to arrest Smith again.

As for other problems . . . .

KICKED OUT AND PUNCHED UP

Wherever Smith went, there were some churches that did not want him in their town. They didn't believe that God would still heal people miraculously today, as He did back in the Early Church times. In fact, some churches in Sweden felt so strongly about Smith that they actually got him kicked out of the country—even though more than 7,000 Swedish people had decided to follow Jesus because of Smith's ministry. God was using Smith to do so many good things, no wonder the demons weren't happy! In fact, of those who were trying to stop Smith's ministry, it was not the police, the churches, or the critical people, it was Satan himself.

Sometimes, Smith would lock himself in a room with a demon-possessed person and attempt to cast out the demon. This made the demon so angry that he would cause the possessed man or woman to bite Smith or punch him. But this didn't scare Smith because God protected him and he just kept on praying until the demon left.

IT'S ONLY THE DEVIL

Smith knew that the devil had no power over him—because Jesus was on his side. One night Smith woke up when he felt an evil presence in his bedroom. When he opened his eyes, he saw Satan standing there. Smith looked at him, said "Oh, it's only you." Then he rolled over and went back to sleep! Smith wasn't scared of the devil. The truth is, the Devil was scared of Smith, because God was with Smith and kept him from all harm. Satan still kept on trying to stop Smith any way he could... but always failed for there was no way he could ever stop Smith Wigglesworth.

One night, Smith stood up to preach. Immediately, he felt something was wrong. "What is it Father?" he prayed. Then he saw a line of people, sitting on a bench and holding hands. God told Smith that these people were praying to the devil, asking him to stop anything good from happening at this church service.

Smith walked over to the bench and lifted up one end of it. He lifted it so high that all of the people slid to the floor. "Get out, you devils!" he shouted. Those people all left as quickly as they could.

Smith knew that the devil was always around trying to stop the good work he was doing for the Lord and he also knew his Bible verses really well. We need to pray and read our Bibles just like Smith did because he remembered in *1st Peter 5:8 the Scripture warns us to: Be sober, be vigilant; because your adversary the devil walks about like a roaring lion, seeking whom he may devour"* and James 4:7 tells us how to make the devil go away: *"Therefore submit to God. Resist the devil and he will flee from you."*

Smith knew that the spiritual world is very real, even though you can't see it or touch it, but he also knew that God's Word was more powerful than anything the devil might try to do and now you and I know it too.

CHAPTER 14

CARRYING REVIVAL "DOWN UNDER"

Not too old to travel

"LET ME TELL YOU ABOUT MY JESUS ..."

In 1922, when Smith was about 63 years old, he travelled a long, long way from home to minister in Australia and New Zealand. He spent several months in these countries, and when he left, many people believed, for the first time, in

God's miraculous power.

During the trip to Australia, the ship stopped in a harbor. The passengers got off the ship and visited a nearby market, where all kinds of strange things were for sale. One of Smith's fellow passengers wanted to buy a big bunch of colorful feathers.

"Hey," the man asked Smith, "do you want to put your money and my money together and buy these feathers?" Now, Smith had no interest in a bunch of feathers. But he felt the Holy Spirit urging him to talk to the man about Jesus. So he agreed to the purchase. However, when it came time to pay for the feathers, the man realized he had left his wallet back on the ship.

"If you will pay the whole cost," the man said, "I promise I will pay you back as soon as we return to the ship. I'll have one of the ship's stewards bring you the money."

"No," Smith replied. "You come and give me the money yourself."

At 10 o'clock the next morning, there was a knock on the door of Smith's cabin.

"Come in!" Smith called.

The man came in with the money for the feathers.

"I don't want your money," Smith told him. "I want your soul. God wants me to talk to you."

For the next 10 minutes, Smith told the man about Jesus. The words brought tears to the man's eyes and before he left Smith's cabin, he had given his life to Jesus.

Smith knew that if they felt Jesus' presence, people would follow Him. He had learned this truth when he started ministering to people. One red-haired boy in the Sunday School did nothing but cause trouble. This kid even smashed out all the windows in the church. But instead of scolding the boy or telling on him, Smith just prayed for him.

A while later, Smith's town had a religious crusade. The crusade seemed to be a flop, however, you never know what God is going to do because that misbehaving boy was one of the few people who were saved and from that moment on, his life changed. He would come and spend hours and hours at Smith's house. He and Smith would sometimes pray late into the night. It seemed that this boy's hunger for God could never be filled. He went on to become a missionary to China, where he spent more than 20 years telling people about Jesus. Smith never forgot how that boy's life was changed.

He loved to see people stirred up to live for God.

POWERFUL PRAYER

In New Zealand, Smith held a prayer meeting with leaders from 10 churches. As Smith prayed, God's presence started to fill the room. This presence was so powerful that it was more than the leaders could handle. One by one, they slipped out of the room, and soon Smith found himself praying alone. A New Zealand pastor named Harry Roberts heard about this episode. "I wouldn't have left that room," he declared.

"I would stay no matter what."

Before long, Pastor Roberts got the chance to live up to his words. Smith held another prayer meeting for church leaders. Roberts attended. Smith started to pray, and God's presence entered the room. It was like a heavy weight on the men's shoulders. It was overwhelming, like it would press them into the floor. People began leaving the room.

Soon, only Pastor Roberts and Smith remained. Pastor Roberts was determined to stay, but, at the same time, he felt like he would die if he stayed much longer.

He was sobbing uncontrollably. God's presence was so strong that he couldn't cope with it. He had to leave the room.

STILL WAITING FOR GOD TO HEAL

Serving God cost Smith a lot. He gave up every moment of every day to do whatever God called him to do. Sometimes this cost was the cruelty of people toward him. For example, some of Smith's enemies made fun of him because he needed glasses. They would mock him, saying, "If God can heal people, why doesn't he heal *you?*"

To make matters worse, Smith's daughter, Alice, was deaf. She needed a "hearing horn" to know what people were saying to her. (A hearing horn is a large hearing aid, shaped like a horn.) Alice's hearing problem made people mock Smith even more. But he was not discouraged. He knew that God was bigger than these problems.

Not *everyone* who was sick or injured was healed in Smith's meetings. Yes, God used Smith to heal many, many people, but healing didn't happen 100 percent of the time. This resulted in some hard questions for Smith. "I believe God will heal my poor eyesight," a man said to Smith. "But should I still wear my glasses?" "If you need them to see, wear them," Smith answered. "Better to be able to see while waiting for God to heal you, than to wander around blind."

Once, Smith was confronted by a woman with diseased gums. After talking with the woman, Smith told her this: "If I were you, I would ask God to either heal you or send you money for a set of false teeth within ten days." The woman followed Smith's advice. Eight days later, she received some unexpected money in the mail. She used it to purchase a set of false teeth. In this case, the solution to the woman's problem did not involve a miraculous healing, but she still received help because she prayed.

TORTURED BY KIDNEY STONES

When Smith reached 70 years of age, he faced one of the hardest challenges of his life.

He began to experience great pain in his stomach area. He prayed, but the pain continued. Finally, things got so bad that Smith visited a doctor. X-rays revealed that Smith had a severe case of kidney stones. Kidney stones are crystals formed by minerals like calcium. These stones, often jagged in shape, can make a person very sick, like they have the flu or food poisoning. Sometimes, the body tries to get rid of these kidney stones when a person urinates. As you can imagine, this process can be extremely painful—and dangerous because it can cause bleeding. After all, urination is meant to get rid of liquid, not hard crystals!

A doctor gave Smith the bad news about his kidney stones: "Your only hope, Mr. Wigglesworth, is for you to have an operation. If you don't, you will die." Smith was direct, as always. "Doctor," he said, "the God who made this body can cure it. No knife will ever cut it as long as I live."

But Smith's pain got worse, not better. One night, he found himself rolling on the floor in agony. He went to the toilet repeatedly, and, one by one, jagged crystals passed out of his body. The pain was blinding!

For quite some time afterward, Smith continued to experience great pain in his stomach area. *Have all of the stones left my body?* he wondered to himself. Smith didn't let the pain affect his ministry. He often preached twice a day. He prayed for hundreds of people's healing, even though he was in agony himself. Smith soon realized that some kidney stones remained in his body. Sometimes he would be praying for people and he would have to stop. He would rush to the restroom to pass another stone, then return to carry on praying.

As we have learned, sometimes passing a kidney stone causes bleeding. So, as time went by, Smith lost so much blood that he became very pale. His body temperature dropped, and he could often be found wrapped in blankets, trying to get warm. This problem lasted for two long and painful years, but Smith was determined to keep ministering.

In the early part of 1932, the 72-year-old Smith asked God, "Please give me fifteen more years to serve you." Somehow, Smith knew God would honor this request, even though he was very sick and he had already lived longer than most healthy men did in the 1930s. He suffered four more years with this pain, then, finally, Smith passed his last stone. He had been saving them in a pot. That pot contained more than 100 kidney stones! Smith had clung to God all this time and now he felt free, free to do God's work in his old age.

CHAPTER 15

A DEATH AT A FUNERAL

Later years

A STRANGE ENCOUNTER

Smith continued to travel all over the world, even though now he was a very old man. He loved to preach God's word. He loved to see Jesus show His true power by doing amazing miracles. Smith ministered throughout Europe, South Africa, and North America. Then he returned home to England.

One day, Smith opened his door to find a young American minister standing there, a newspaper tucked under his arm. The young man introduced himself as Lester Sumrall.

"You can't come in here with that," Smith said, pointing at the newspaper. "Throw it away." (Remember, the Bible was the only reading material that Smith allowed in his home.) Lester shoved the paper into some nearby bushes and followed Smith inside.

Smith had been reading the Bible when Lester Sumrall came knocking, so he invited the young minister to listen while he read God's Word aloud for about a half hour. Then Smith said, "Let's pray. Smith finished his prayer by blessing Lester. This prayer was followed by *another* half hour of Bible reading, then more prayer. Finally, the two men shared a meal, prepared by Alice, who was helping to care for her aging father. When the meal was over, Smith put down his napkin. "Come back again sometime," he said. Then he walked out of the room. Alice led the puzzled young pastor to the front door. Lester thanked her for the meal and walked away.

This encounter with Smith Wigglesworth had been strange, but, still, Lester sensed that God had done something inside him. He felt different. After that encounter, Lester

Sumrall was a frequent guest at the Wigglesworth home. Each time was just as strange as the first.

In 1939, when the Second World War started, Lester had to return to his home in America. He went to see Smith one last time. Smith started to cry as he prayed a final blessing on Lester.

"I see a great revival coming," Smith said. "Dead people will be raised up, and many people will come to know Jesus. I'm not going to see this with my eyes, but you will!" As Smith prayed and wept, Lester wept and prayed with him. Smith served God right to the end of his life.

IT'S TIME TO GO HOME

One day, he told Alice, "Today in my mail, I have been invited to go to Australia, India, Sri Lanka, and America. People everywhere are looking to me." Then he started to cry. "Poor me!" he said. "What a failure I am. To think that people have their eyes on *me*. God will never share His glory with anyone; He will take them from the scene."

Seven days later, Smith traveled to a dear friend's funeral. As the car drove to the church, Smith told his fellow passengers that he felt wonderful. He pointed out places he and Polly had preached and described the miracles Jesus had done in each place. When he got to the church, he saw the father of a young girl that he had prayed for just a few days earlier. The girl had been dying. "Well, how's your daughter?" Smith asked.

The man hesitated, "She is a little better," he offered. "She is having less pain." Smith was crushed. He had expected to hear of the girl's complete healing. His heart broke for her. He sighed deeply. Then Smith bowed his head. Peacefully and with no pain, he went to Heaven to be with Jesus. The day was March 12, 1947.

SMITH'S LIFE WITH GOD

Smith Wigglesworth lived his life for God. He was a rough, uneducated man. Many people thought that God couldn't use him—or shouldn't use him. But Smith loved God, and that is what matters most. He spent his life growing closer to God and living for God.

As we have seen time after time, Smith also loved people. In fact, the closer he got to God, the more he loved people. God used him to show other people what could happen if they would only believe in Him. This belief is more than just saying some words. It is truly believing in God in your heart. Believing no matter what happens in life. Everything Smith knew, he learned from the Bible. It was the only book he read. God can use you in the same way, if you are willing to seek Him with all your heart and believe what is written in the Bible.

Take a step of faith and act on what it says in the Bible, and then see what God does. Like Smith, you can grow one step at a time. You can do great things for God in this world. Smith is now in Heaven but the Holy Spirit is still here on Earth, looking for people like Smith Wigglesworth that He can use in big ways.

You could be one of them.

BIBLE STUDY FOR YOUNG GENERALS

Read Matthew 21:18-22.

1. List some of the amazing things that Jesus did when He was on earth.

2. Think about what you've read in this book. What are the most amazing things that happened in Smith Wigglesworth's life?

3. Verse 21 above tells us we have to have something if we want to see God do amazing things. What is it?

4. Verse 21 also tells us about something that we must *not* do. What is it?

5. What happens when you pray and believe God can answer (see verse 22)?

6. Is there something that God wants you to pray about? Why don't you pray about it now and trust God that He will answer your prayers.

SMITH WIGGLESWORTH— ACTIVITY SECTION

REMEMBER THE BOOK

How much of the story can you remember? Test your memory by answering these questions.

Answers are given on page 121.

1. What country did Smith live in?
2. What was Smith's wife called?
3. Where did Smith meet his wife?
4. How did Smith witness to people on the boat to America?
5. When Smith hit the man with stomach cancer, who thought the man had been killed?
6. What illness did Smith suffer from when he was 70?

CHOOSE THE RIGHT ANSWER

Answers are given on page 121.

1. How old was Smith when he had his first job?

   A. 6

   B. 8

   C. 16

2. What did Smith ask God for when he started to preach full time?

   A. Lots of money

   B. Smart clothes

   C. A bigger Bible

3. What was Smith's last job before he became a preacher?

   A. A carpenter

   B. A doctor

   C. A plumber

4. What did God tell Smith to do to help him remember things?

   A. Pray

   B. Say them out loud

   C. Write them down

5. When the devil came into Smith's bedroom, what did Smith do?
   A. Get up and pray
   B. Roll over and sleep
   C. Call a friend
6. What did Smith Wigglesworth die of?
   A. Old age
   B. Cancer
   C. Food poisoning

ANSWERS

1. England, 2. Polly (this was her nickname, her actual name was Mary Jane), 3. In the Salvation Army, 4. He sang a song, 5. The man's doctor, 6. Kidney stones.

1. A, 2. B, 3. C, 4. C, 5. B, 6. A.

AROUND THE WORLD

Smith travelled to lots of places. Time yourself to find out how quickly can you find these countries on a world map in the order they are written:

1. America
2. Australia
3. England
4. India
5. New Zealand
6. Norway
7. South Africa
8. Switzerland

Write down your times here.

Date	Time Taken

PUZZLE IT

Find these ten words in the word search.

1. Smith
2. Polly
3. England
4. Believe
5. Healing

6. Tongues
7. Holy Spirit
8. Preach
9. Souls
10. Boldness

O	P	H	E	A	L	I	N	G	N
T	B	O	L	D	N	E	S	S	E
P	O	L	L	S	L	I	Y	L	V
R	L	Y	P	O	K	D	P	N	E
E	B	S	E	U	G	N	O	T	I
A	D	P	M	L	T	A	L	G	L
C	S	I	E	S	L	L	L	D	E
H	I	R	J	B	G	G	Y	E	B
S	M	I	T	H	E	N	Q	K	N
V	E	T	S	M	I	E	S	S	E

FIND IT OUT

In chapter 4 we read that Smith had to work hard as a plumber during a cold winter.

Why would a cold winter make a plumber work harder? (If you're not sure, read chapter 4 again).

Try this experiment to see how water expands when you freeze it.

YOU WILL NEED

- Kitchen scales
- Two identical small cups
- Water
- Cooking oil
- A freezer

WHAT TO DO

1. Take a small cup and fill it up to the top with water.
2. Fill another cup with oil.

3. Weigh each cup (don't forget to write down what they weigh).

4. Place both cups in the freezer and leave them to freeze.

5. When the oil and water have frozen, which cup looks like it has more in it?

6. Weigh the cups again. Has the weight changed?

QUESTIONS TO THINK ABOUT

1. Has the weight changed?

2. Has anything been added or taken away from the cups?

3. Has the volume changed?

4. What can happen to a pipe if water freezes inside it?

FOR FURTHER RESEARCH

See if you can find out why water expands when it freezes.

YOUR TURN

In chapter 7 we read that Smith started to speak in tongues. The local newspaper wrote about Smith's experience. Imagine you were the local reporter. Write the newspaper report of what happened. Type it up and include a photo of Smith Wigglesworth.

GET CREATIVE

Create a poster with pictures of all the miracles mentioned in chapters 11 and 12.

AUTHORS' NOTE TO READERS AND PARENTS

Like Smith Wigglesworth, I believe that God can cure people miraculously today. Unlike Mr. Wigglesworth, I do *not* believe that this is the only way that God will work. God gives wisdom and knowledge to us to help us fight disease. Medicine has advanced much since the time of Smith Wigglesworth. Medical care can actually be part of God's plan for bringing relief and healing to His people. However, medicine still does not hold all the answers. I am in favor of both competent medical treatment and the power of prayer. I would not encourage anyone to neglect either of these at their time of need.

BIBLIOGRAPHY

Stanley Howard Frodsham, *Smith Wigglesworth: Apostle of Faith* (Springfield, MO: Gospel Publishing House, 1948)

Roberts Liardon, *Go✦'s Generals: Why They Succee✦e✦ an✦ Why Some Faile✦* (Tulsa, OK: Whitaker House 1996)

Roberts Liardon, *Smith Wigglesworth: The Complete Collection of His Life Teachings* (Tulsa, OK: Albury Publishing 1996)

Julian Wilson, *Wigglesworth: The Complete Story* (Colorado Springs, CO: Authentic 2004)

AUTHORS' CONTACT INFORMATION

ROBERTS LIARDON

Roberts Liardon Ministries, United States office:

P.O. Box 781888, Orlando, FL 32878

E-mail: Info1@robertsliardon.org

www.robertsliardon.org

United Kingdom/European office:

Roberts Liardon Ministries

22 Notting Hill Gate, Suite 125

London W11 3JE, UK

OLLY GOLDENBERG

BM Children Can, London WC1N 3XX, UK

info@childrencan.co.uk

www.childrencan.co.uk

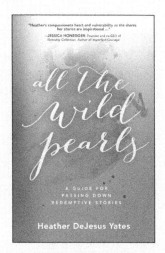

Made in the USA
Las Vegas, NV
12 May 2022

48790284R00083